D0821856

THE PLAYGOER'S HANDBOOK TO THE
ENGLISH RENAISSANCE DRAMA

THE PLAYGOER'S HANDBOOK

TO THE

ENGLISH RENAISSANCE DRAMA

By

AGNES MURE MACKENZIE,

M.A., D.Litt.

Author of *The Women in Shakespeare's Plays,* etc.

NEW YORK

COOPER SQUARE PUBLISHERS, INC.

1971

Originally Published 1927
Published 1971 by Cooper Square Publishers, Inc.
59 Fourth Avenue, New York, N. Y. 10003
International Standard Book No. 0-8154-0373-9
Library of Congress Catalog Card No. 75-145871

Printed in the United States of America

CONTENTS

PREFACE

'I would rather say true things than new things. If the true are also new, it is not my fault.'
The Autobiography of a Writer of No Importance.

To many people, of recent years, the drama of the Elizabethans has been a highbrow cult. The highbrows are now moving on to the Restoration and the Russians, where they will find a more congenial grazing-ground than in the virile work of Marlowe, Chapman, or Shakespeare : and the rightful audience of the Old Vic must feel a little like the owners of a great country house who watch, on a bank-holiday evening, the exit of the final char-à-bancs. Yet still, to many who might care for it, the Elizabethan drama remains a perplexing and fantastic form of *literature*, raved over, or alternatively at, by critics who treat it as anything in the world but a body of stage-plays.

A good play, of course – to say nothing of some bad ones like *Paracelsus* – is literature. So am I a ratepayer. But both the play and I are some other things as well. And of these things, in the Elizabethan play's case, most people seem to be trained out of cognizance, just as the children of last generation were carefully trained out of any sense of rhythm in poetry. I have, frankly, no great qualifications for retraining them. Only I care a good deal about the theatre: I like some very varied kinds of play: and it is perhaps as well that there should be humble people who do not mind doing anything so obvious as considering a large body of drama, already acted and written to be acted, in terms of the theatre and not the university class-room, the Café Royal, or a political crossword puzzle. So I have tried to write of these plays primarily as drama.

9

For brotherhood's sake I should like to feel this book might be of service to an undergraduate, especially in the Dramatic Society rather than the examination-hall. I should be still more pleased if it were useful to a dramatic critic, though I fear that those whose criticisms show most confusion on its subject are unlikely to admit there is anything they need to learn. But the people for whom it is really written are those like myself, plain men and women without claim to scholarship and with a considerable objection to highbrows and such vermin of the arts, who love 'the humanities' in all their forms, both those familiar and those that through an unfamiliar idiom bring the voice of men who regard things that matter to ourselves.

ST JOHN'S WOOD, 1926

'Great drama can only live when it is acted.'

NIGEL PLAYFAIR, *The Story of the Lyric Theatre*.

'There are three stages:

'(1) All 16th-century literature seems confused, foolishly quaint, and ignorant. This is the view of the uneducated public. *Ye Olde Curyosytee Shoppe*.

'(2) All 16th-century literature seems fresh, admirably quaint, and original. This is the view of the educated public.

'(3) At this dizzy height, 16th-century literature exactly resembles 19th-century literature in that it is both good and bad, although all the writers use variants of the same modes of speech.'

SIR WALTER RALEIGH *in a letter*.

CHAPTER ONE

THE ELIZABETHAN PLAY

'Their alleged lack of proportion.'
JOHN BUCHAN, *Homilies and Recreations.*

'We are not to seek for every sort of pleasure from a tragedy, but only for that which is proper to the species.'
ARISTOTLE, *The Poetics.*

✱

A CRITIC of the last generation would have denied with emphasis that there could be anything approaching form or coherence in a play with twenty-eight changes of scene, which is the number in the printed text of *Antony and Cleopatra.* But in the last twenty years we have learnt several things about the theatre. One is that there are two quite different methods of mounting plays: and both of them are right. And the discovery of that has led us to discover that there are several different ways of constructing plays, and more than one of them is quite 'legitimate.'

A play off the stage is not a play at all, but merely the words and stage-directions of one, which are to the whole what the skeleton and the voice are to a person. So let us begin where the rediscovery began, with the mounting, the way in which a play is put upon the stage. Take *Ghosts* and *Quality Street,* and consider how they should be 'set.' Sharply contrasted as they are, they have one point in common: both, obviously, ask that the stage should give the illusion of an actual room in an actual place and time: the producer must endeavour to represent as closely as possible Fru Alving's parlour or Miss Throssel's Blue Room. An extreme example is a play like *Milestones* or *Secrets,* where a lot of the dramatic

13

point is precisely in the minute reproduction of the room where the action is supposed to pass: the drawing-room in *Milestones* is one of the dramatis personæ. The realistic method of last century, with its practicable doors, its elaborate furnishings and wealth of detail, is the proper one for plays that set out to reproduce the surface of life with realism, to give their author's meaning through the speech and gesture of everyday, in the same key as we experience them.

But there is another kind of drama, whose appeal is different, and which demands for itself a different kind of staging if that appeal is not to be confused. Here the décor, costume apart, has for its purpose not to create an illusion which shall be as much a part of the play as the actor's make-up: what it does is to form a background to the actors, which will remain mere background, related to the play as a frame is related to a picture – essential to it, helping it (no artist will show an unframed picture if he can avoid it) but never part of it and never calling attention to itself, even by beauty.[1] The result is the kind of décor with which producers like Mr. Poel, Mr. Playfair, and Mr. Atkins, designers like Mr. Lovat Fraser, Mr. Shelving, Mr. Garside, and Mr. Rickett have familiarized us. The scenery is not part of the play, and is not meant to be. It is simply there to set it off.

Now, nobody who has seen Shakespeare played in the tradition of the Lyceum and in that of the Old Vic can doubt which of the two types is that belonging to his kind of drama. As a matter of fact it is the only one that is physically possible

[1] It may sound absurd to speak of the settings of *St. Joan, The Immortal Hour,* and *The Beggar's Opera* as 'not calling attention to themselves.' But I have expressly excluded costume from this context; and divorced from costume, the stage sets in all these plays were of the simplest – which is not to say, of course, that they were easily contrived.

if we are to present his plays, with their intricate supple form, as he intended them. A play is not merely the representation of a series of events. It is a significant pattern made out of certain phases of these events, in such a way that, witnessing it, we see their meaning: and you cannot monkey with the pattern without destroying it and some part of the meaning with it, any more than you can cut Velazquez' *King Philip* into bits with a knife, shuffle the result, and say you have Velazquez' picture. We have long praised Shakespeare as a poet and a psychologist. It was just, for he is supremely great as either. It is one of the things that will stand to the credit of a century with much need of its virtues that we are beginning to realize also that he was no less magnificent a playwright, that to cut about and disintegrate the splendid orchestrations of the action in *Antony and Cleopatra* is like saying that it does not matter if we hang the Discobolos' leg over his shoulder, or omit alternate bars of a Bach chorale.

For our present purposes, the rediscovery amounts to this. We have realized that there is more than one kind of dramatic idiom, and that certain kinds of play can take, or rather demand, ways of production that are not necessarily those of Sir Henry Irving, or necessarily those of Mr. Gordon Craig. And having reached that point of view, it is easy to see, as converse, that a theatre very unlike Irving's Lyceum would grow plays that were equally unlike Sir Arthur Pinero's, with a quite different set of dramatic conventions – different, but not necessarily either better or worse.

With these things in our minds, let us look at the Elizabethan play and its theatre. The two are, in their essence, indivisible. You cannot have an art without its material media – paper and ink, sound, paint, or marble, the actors and their theatre. And these media will to a large extent condition the possibilities of their art. If you are very clever, or do not mind depending on the catalogue, you may *suggest* a sunset in a bas-relief: but you will probably find it more natural to leave that sort of subject to the painter. Or if you are a very great artist indeed, you may get the 'feel' of the sunset into your bas-relief, in such a way that you have permanently enlarged the possibilities of the medium, as those men did who, discovering perspective, gave two-dimensional painting a third dimension.

Both these things happened in the English Renaissance drama. It was conditioned by its medium, by the kind of theatre – and audience – that were possible. And it permanently enlarged the possibilities of English dramatic form. It was not, of course, in itself an entirely new thing. There had been, on the one side, the very popular dramatic entertainments descended from the liturgy of the Church: and on the other there were the great plays of that antiquity that was passionately the intellectual fashion. When in the hands of men whose background was both theatre and university, the two streams met, there were Marlowe and Peele, and the English Renaissance play in being, to be suppled and enriched, enlarged in scope, coloured by the personality, the varying technical skill, of different men, weakened eventually into decadence: but very little changed in essence, until the far side of the Restoration.

The general conditions of the thing, on the whole, were these. You had a company of actors, trained to speak verse, to make the most of face and voice and gesture, and so accustomed to continual changes of rôle that it must have been difficult to grow mechanical. They had, as setting, a stage that gave them no help in the way of lighting – a very important aid emotionally – and none normally from suggestive background, or even from the pictorial element involved in grouping, since the actors were not set within the frame of a proscenium, but on a projecting stage with the audience on three sides of them, and sometimes even on the fourth as well.

The sole visual appeal then must be by gesture, in the widest sense, and costume. They were not neglected. The Elizabethan and Jacobean plays are full of action, even violent action : δρᾶμα, *drama*, the thing done, is always at the core of them,[1] however Hamlet or Bussy may philosophize. The rhythmical movement of the body comes in too at times as decoration, as in dancing, skilled swordsmanship, and the innumerable ordered processions that enter and withdraw to the sound of trumpets. Costume, again, was very rich and splendid: the magnificence of the wardrobe was made easier by the fact that men, as they had always done in the Middle Ages,[2] saw the action they were presenting as if it were contemporary with themselves, and so experienced it: and therefore wore representing it the dress of their own day, that expressed so perfectly its arrogant and splendid spirit. The point, to-day, is worth remembering, for dress, like speech, grows naturally from the temperament of a period. To give *Hamlet* or *Macbeth*, the very essence of their age, in the garments of the *Nibelungenlied* – or *The Forsyte Saga* – is as absurd æsthetically as to put Vivie Warren into a cote-hardie or translate *The Faerie Queene* into the language of *The Daily Mail*. And if you think that the translation does not matter, you had

---

[1] At the core at least of plays intended for the public theatre. A court-play like *Endymion* or *Love's Labour's Lost* may be as purely 'drama of discussion' as *Getting Married*.

[2] Cf. Chaucer's *Troylus and Creseyde* and *The Knightes Tale*. The Greek stories are made purely mediæval, and Duke Theseus might easily be John of Gaunt.

B

better send this book back to the library at once. It is wasting
your time.

If the visual possibilities were limited, they were, so far as
they went, fairly intense. Clear, violent action, gorgeous costume, gesture: they used them all, and so it would seem,
lavishly. But the main appeal was rather to ear than eye. The
dramatic vehicle was double-sided: on one the action, on the
other the great verse that elucidated it and gave it an orches-
tration of emotions. The play was the thing: and a play as
such is neither words nor acts, but *both*, fused into an insepar-
able unity.

Finally, for the last of the governing conditions, there was
the audience. Not – very much not – twentieth-century
Chelsea: not twentieth-century Oxford, Mayfair, or Poplar,
Sheffield or Surbiton, but London at the turn of 1600, which
was not externally like any of these. It was a full-blooded
age. It liked the elementary animal instincts, fighting and sex
and feeding, but liked them in the main without self-consciousness, though it could be very acutely conscious of its
own experience of them – a rather different thing. It took for
granted the high-coloured expression of these experiences, and
of more subtle ones, not only in art but in life. These fiery
loves and hates, these lurid complicated vengeances, really did
happen in Renaissance London, still more in Renaissance
Edinburgh or Paris, still more again, with a gay taken-for-
granted callousness, in Renaissance Venice or Milan or
Naples. To climb the marvellous great stair at Blois, where
the stones laugh with intricate lovely traceries, and remember
Guise mounting through those new carvings to sudden bloody
death by the King's bed, is to understand some things about
the older drama that seem far-fetched in an atmosphere of
class-rooms. It was a greedy, vivid age – greedy for all experi-

ence, of mind or body, and greediest of all for the spirit's that outranges either. The passionate hunger of the mind and spirit caused a passionate sensitiveness to what best reveals their shifts and turnings, language. No age has ever had such joy in words, such subtle quick awareness of them. In spite of the desire for violent action, drama could make its way on talk alone, even, on the swift tennis-play of word and meaning. The intricate punning that we now find tedious was a game to them, a game of skill to be delighted in. They relished John Lyly's sentences as we delight in Mademoiselle Lenglen.

Every one loved the theatre, except the Puritans. It was the national amusement. And it had to appeal to a very varied lot of people. Shakespeare could catch them all at once — philosophers and poets and the limbs of Limehouse, though it is true that the highbrows were rather superior. *Hamlet* and *Othello* are first-class melodramas. Cut out the poetry and the psychology, strip off the verse, and put them on in Surreyside English at the Elephant and Castle, and you would have a happy audience. That is why Shakespeare made a comfortable fortune: and why the highbrow of all ages has always been inclined to patronize him. Few men had the skill for that, though. They wrote for one audience or the other, or if they condescended to the one they were not writing for, it was by inserting irrelevant slabs of perfunctory low-comedy, or making the gore run flagrantly thick and slab. Sometimes, of course, like Lyly, they could write for the Court alone, for a court where a man needed letters as he needed horsemanship or table manners: and then idea and whimsical conceit, poetry and inventiveness of dialogue, have a free hand, and are consequently a little decayed now, for ideas 'date' far sooner than emotion. But it is interesting to note that although one does sometimes get these qualities without action, one very rarely gets action alone without at least the attempt to get beyond it, to appeal, however crudely, to imagination, even to intellect. Ophelia, who was not a woman of letters, and had not a very intelligent mind in any case, admires Hamlet's scholarship as she does his swordplay, bracketing both with his accomplished courtiership. The Elizabethan courtier would have blushed at a literary solecism as fervently as at whatever was the Elizabethan equivalent for wearing brown boots with a top hat. Men rose politically on the strength of a well-turned sonnet: and it seemed as natural that they should as it does to us that they should rise on a successful deal in cocoa. The political result was perhaps the same.

Now the plays produced under these conditions were obviously bound to vary, as all individual specimens of a live art must. At the same time they were also bound to have some things in common, especially as regards fundamental form, which in any art must be conditioned by its medium – a term which, in the widest sense, includes its audience, for a thing is not expressed until the expression has been experienced objectively.

The two chief common points are a certain emphasis laid upon diction, and a freedom, to us very remarkable and at first bewildering, regarding structure. And for a third thing, realism was difficult, at any rate for long at a time and seriously. Do without scenery, accept from the classics and the Mysteries that verse was the natural medium for serious drama, and you were pretty well cut off from that.

But the absence of scenery gave extraordinary freedom. When you needed nothing but the dialogue to give you Rome or Alexandria, then you could have Antony in the one followed immediately by five minutes or so of Cæsar in the other, to serve as commentary and bring out its point. The result is a form that within its limits of length is nearly as flexible as the novelist's. Our typical modern drama in, say, three acts of a single scene apiece, must run its action like a melody. A play like *Antony and Cleopatra*, with nearly thirty scenes instead of three, can orchestrate, working elaborate harmonies of action on different planes, in a manner so subtle that to the unfamiliar *reader* it seems inchoate and confusing, but that straightens and clarifies at once if we see it acted.

It is perhaps easier for us to take in the harmonics of Shakespeare's construction in that our age has native to it a dramatic art structurally (if not otherwise) parallel, the cinema. Here again we have perfect freedom as regards change of place, and the result is a flexibility of lay-out, a freedom in the use of juxtaposed elements as parallels and contrasts, that gives a technique of construction, of the patterning of a story, quite different from that of the play limited to three or four scenes at the outside. That it is seldom really used, often abused, is true: but that does not abolish its value as a means of expression to anyone who can use it.

This freedom, like all other liberty, needs vigilance. The freer an art is, the bigger need to be the men who practise it. The ultimate test of good breeding is to be able to lounge without sprawling: and the ultimate test of art, on the formal side, is to be able to use an elastic medium fully, but without shapelessness. Few men can do it: few of the Elizabethans did. In form even more than in psychological range and penetration, Shakespeare towers over them. He alone, perhaps, until Beaumont and Fletcher, *consciously* realized the problems of structure in his medium as it lay to his hand, without the hankering after alien conditions that we see in Jonson, another deliberate and conscious artist. It took him a little time to learn – not very long, though, for *Midsummer Night's Dream*, very early in his work, and *Romeo and Juliet*, about the same time, are excellently put together. There are occasions, of course, even in late work, where he lets himself be unpardonably careless. From the structural point of view, *Cymbeline* is sheerly slovenly: I could have made a better job of it myself. When he is really working, though, he is superb, in this as in all other qualities. However it may irritate those people who dare not for their lives be in the majority, it is the simple fact that he is not merely head and shoulders above the rest, but head and body. Yet he is so great that even then they are not small.

It is true, all the same, that in form they are not always capable of their freedom. Still, to recognize that their form is often faulty is very different from saying they have none. There is often madness in their method, but fundamentally it is 'a good method, by very much more handsome than fine.' It may not be better than the method of *Hedda Gabler*, any more than painting is better than sculpture, or vice versa. Both kinds have an equal right to exist, as Ibsen knew a good deal clearlier than his prophets. What are *Brand* and *Peer Gynt* but uncommonly successful uses of it? And *Peer Gynt* stages admirably, when the Old Vic does it with ten years of unmutilated Shakespeare to teach its company to go about it.

Construction is one point, then. The other is diction – the rushing gorgeous verse, the frequent word-play, those long soliloquies that (we used to be told) 'impede the action.' Do you grumble when Tristran sings an aria? Or when Pavlova's entry drops the ballet to mere background for her solo?

The Elizabethan drama comes rather close to parts of Wagner's dream, of music and drama fused into a unity, each quickening, interpreting, the other. The music here is the music not of instruments, but that music in the thought that we call poetry, expressed in the voice of a man speaking in verse – doing something, that is, that is neither speaking nor singing, but a blend of both, and consequently as distinct from either as purple is distinct from red or blue. Unless one can postulate an audience trained to swallow, even to like, poetry, as we have been trained to find intelligible, even platitudinous, the Wagner that was an outrage to our grandfathers, one need not bother about Elizabethan drama. I am not speaking as the superior person. Poetry is as natural to man as dancing is, or meditation: only in modern cities we are trained out of capacity for any real achievement in these three, and must retrain ourselves, not without labour, and alas, not, sometimes, without priggishness.

An easily accessible instance of the parallel with opera comes in the opening scene of *Midsummer Night's Dream*. The lovers' situation has been sketched in dialogue – in dialogue that is fairly realistic in key, though verse. Then the court leave them alone, and . . . in opera, obviously, there would be an aria. And so there is, only it is in elaborate rhymed verse, not music.

The importance of this poetic element varies, of course, from play to play. Sometimes, as in the extreme case of *Tamburlaine*, the thing is one huge lyric, orchestrated between many voices, illustrated at times by violent, half-symbolic action, but in itself pure poetry – the poetry is what the thing is there for. To complain that it is a bad play is like objecting to *The Magic Flute* because it does not use the technique of *The Doctor's Dilemma*. At the other extreme, in, say, *Arden of Feversham*, the verse is merely equivalent to the 'incidental music' of the old-fashioned melodrama: action is what matters, and the poetry is used (not very skilfully as a rule) to emphasize it. Between these two come any Elizabethan play. A critic may be bored by the long speeches of the Duke of Biron. He is quite entitled to be bored by them. But he is not entitled to blame Chapman for putting them in: he had a right, in turn, to use them, if he chose, in the kind of thing that he was trying to make. They are as much a part of his material as the stage or the actors, and though there is no reason why one should not prefer the modern tragedy whose protagonists converse in an alternation of grunts and silences, that is not to call Chapman's method illegitimate.

CHAPTER TWO

SHAKESPEARE'S PREDECESSORS

MEDIÆVAL DRAMA. THE CLASSICAL REVIVAL. THE
EARLY RENAISSANCE DRAMA. FOUR NOTABLE
PLAYS OF THE MID-CENTURY

'There was no art in the world till by experience found out.'
GEORGE PUTTENHAM, *Art of English Poesy.*

★

So far I have spoken of the Elizabethan play as of one particular kind of dramatic art, laying stress on the points in which
one play resembles its neighbours, and both differ from those
of the twentieth century. It is needful now to look at them
individually. Ford and Ben Jonson seem to have much in
common if you come to them just after *The Silver Box.* Yet
they are no more alike, fundamentally, than Oscar Wilde and
Mr. Bernard Shaw, both Irishmen who wrote prose comedies
in the early nineties of last century.

The plays that we know as 'the Elizabethan drama' did not
begin to be written until Elizabeth herself had reigned some
quarter of a century:[1] yet from the beginning of her reign, and
for three centuries at least before it, there had been a drama of
some kind in England, and its nature helped to determine that
which followed it. The Elizabethan theatre, too, foreran the
'Elizabethan play' by about a decade, and again did much to
condition the work of the men who made that play precisely
what it was. It will be as well, therefore, to consider briefly

[1] Most of the greatest, too, come in the reign of her successor. Yet in
those greatest there is more of the spirit of her reign than of his, so I
have not attempted to break up the popular classification by severing 'the
Jacobeans.'

25

what these preliminaries were like, before we come to deal with the greater work that grew from them.

Wherever there is drama, the beginnings of it are in religious ceremony. The drama of Western Europe is no exception: the Mass, the central act of the international Church, is, among many other things, a play. Something significant is *done*, in a pre-appointed mode and order, and elucidated by an accompanying and appointed form of words, by a body of men who have their appointed parts and represent something more than their personal individualities – the priest, vested for Mass, is no longer Father Brown-Jones, but the Celebrant. And these things are done and said in the presence of, and for, a larger body, visible and invisible, which is recognized as co-operant in them by its very presence – the French word for hearing Mass is still *assister*. The Mass has thus the characteristics of drama, both representational and expressionist. It has, and is, much more than that, of course: but it is that among the other things.

The representational side was obviously edifying to a mediæval congregation, that being illiterate must be taught by other means than the newspapers that compulsory education has made the chief influence (with the film, of course) on the popular mind of our own day: and so it strengthened. A mediæval church, from crypt to spire, was one vast picturebook, and the pictures soon came alive and appeared in the services. There were Our Lady and St. John already, flanking the Rood, carved out of wood or stone: why not bring them down to speak and act as in the great incidents of the Faith – on Easter morning make the folk *see* Easter, by dressing up three servers as the Maries, and letting the congregation see them find the Empty Tomb? Of course it was neces-

sary for them to have words to show who they were, and
express what they were doing and experiencing. Hence came
the *Tropes*, semi-dramatic additions to the Liturgy for special
occasions, by the mere natural extension of such symbolic
rites as the deposition of the altar cross upon Good Friday, or
the Franciscan device of the Christmas crib: and very soon
they enlarged into the *Mysteries*, that gave a detailed representation in speech and action of the great incidents in the
history of Mansoul.

The people loved them: before very long they were doing
them themselves. Just as a craft guild or any other corporate
body in that age of corporations and sodalities might offer a
painted window in honour of its patron saint, so it would
offer a representation of his life in action, instead of in paint or
glass or carving in wood and stone. And naturally they found
it tremendous fun. It became a regular part of any holiday.

The holiday spirit is strong, too. Odd as it may sound to
modern pleasure-seekers, as to the adherents of some modern
religions, these people really did feel joy in reminding themselves that the Universe was governed by a Power which loved
them to the point of putting on mortality for their sake, and
suffering death and sorrow and the consciousness of failure for
them. It was a piece of good news, an *evangelium*, that stood a
lot of repetition, and affected life in general just as the news of
the Armistice did. So although from one point of view it was
a thing to sober men and make them walk humbly, as the discovery of a great love will make anyone, from another it
turned them naturally to gaiety. And when normal men are
cheerful, they make jokes.

They did. They looked at the Nativity in a mood of cheerful festival. And when they saw it in the story approached by
folk like themselves, folk like Diccon over the hill or Alice's

brother, they put in Diccon and Alice's brother as they saw
them, with a cheery take-off of the way they grumbled at the
weather or the taxes. It made it much more real, too. And
when they had in Herod and the other villains of the piece,
they guyed them. It was great fun: and the writers would get
out of it that strange intense delight in having got something
down, in having pinned and made permanent some fleeting
instant of vivid experience, that is perhaps the basic motive of
all artists.

✓   By the end of the fourteenth century – by Chaucer's time,
that is – these plays of the traditions of the Church, from Bible
and Saints' lives, were well established: and an integral and
taken-for-granted part of them was this element of ordinary
human life, including the humour of it. Then, by that time,
there is beginning to be an extension. From the *Romance of
the Rose* onward – that is to say, from the mid thirteenth century – allegory had been immensely popular. At the root of
all Catholic metaphysic and practice lies a strong sense that
life is *sacramental*, that matter is the vehicle of spirit, and
neither, in the world perceptible to man, can operate apart
from the other – a point of view which is very much that of
the most modern physical science, with its insistence that
matter is merely a series of expressions of pure energy, and
which is as remote as possible from any sense of an essential
hostility between matter and spirit as such – an idea which in
fact was pungently and recurrently condemned by the Church
as manichæism. This 'sacramental' outlook on life naturally
gives rise to a strong sense of the symbolic: and as result,
allegory and allegorical interpretation of anything from history to mathematics was one of the intellectual crazes of the
time: Dante made the *Divine Comedy* out of it, and the
second-rate men made of it what the second-rate always do

when an intellectual idea becomes fashionable, as witness our
recent burst of Freudian fiction. In a while it occurred to
somebody to dramatize it: and then there was a new form, the
Morality. It suffered, coming when it did, from the awful
wordiness that cursed the fifteenth century: it is generally
portentously dull. But it marks a real advance for all that, for
now at last there exists a vernacular drama whose action, as
well as dialogue, is invented. Plays were dividing, too, into
different types. Things like the shrewd humorous realism of
the Shepherds episode in the famous Towneley Nativity Play
were splitting off to form the *Interludes* – rough little
'sketches,' often gaily satirical, where the official point might
still be some pious principle, or, very soon, a piece of politico-
religious propaganda, but the real one, in the main, was knock-
about fun. These were being taken up, too, by the professional entertainers, the singers, reciters, acrobats, and dancers,
who had existed all through the Middle Ages. And since the
reputation of these people and the general level of their characters were as a rule neither saintly nor dignified, it was not
the graver elements they strengthened. The amateurs still
played, of course: amateur acting was one of the great amusements of all society until the Civil War of the mid-seventeenth
century. The dignified bodies – Corporations honouring a
royal visit, the Inns of Court, the Universities, held to the
dignified forms on the whole, of course. But the distinction is
not clearly cut. University students might, and did, play the
more solemn moralities, and play them with a serious interest
too, for the undergraduate (a person who alters very little
through the ages) is usually keen enough on ethical and theo-
logical ideas. But also, then as now, he enjoyed a rag, especially if it involved a good-natured slap at the dignity of digni-
taries. So the universities also played interludes, and conversely

the professional entertainers made capital with the respectable by staging pieces of impeccable moral and most pious diction.

There are two more new forms growing alongside these. The Renaissance inherited all the mediæval delight in pageantry – in pageantry to take the ear as well as the eye; so there developed the *Masque*, pure pageantry for its own sake, of poetry, music, movement, and rich dress, held together by some thin thread of occasionally recollected idea, in much the fashion of a musical comedy.[1] It was costly, for splendour was part of the game, so it was confined to Court or the sub-courts of wealthy nobles, or to rich corporations like the universities or the Inns. It was immensely fashionable, right up to the Civil War: and it had a very strong influence upon the development of staging, for since a lavish display was an integral part of it, elaborate mechanical devices were contrived, machines and lighting and costly backgrounds, scenic and other, that greatly enhanced the resources of the naked stage, especially as plays written for court performance, like *The Tempest* and (probably) *Macbeth*, came naturally to be enriched with elaborate mechanical devices, that were not yet possible in the ordinary theatre. But this is overrunning my present period. By the death of Henry VIII, there were several dramatic forms established and popular – mystery, miracle, and morality for edification, masque for pageantry, and interlude in the main for amusement unimpaired by instruction, though like its narrative analogue the fabliau it could be used, and was, for purposes of propaganda. And the scholars were rediscovering the classics.

Particularly, they rediscovered Seneca. Seneca was a

[1] Milton's *Comus* in 1634 is on the whole typical, though there is rather more story and less decoration than usual.

Roman dramatist of the first century, and like nearly all Roman artists, thought he was copying the Greeks. The result, in his case, rather reminds one of the German courts which tried to copy Versailles. He left out the poetry of Greek drama, vulgarized its high philosophy, and enhanced and elaborated the more lurid elements in the barbaric myths on which its action had been based. Yet, since Seneca was indubitably a classic, he was a respectable person to imitate. Imitate him, and you were classical, and therefore in the mode: and if your personal tastes led you to imitate his gory revenges rather than his elaborate diction, you were still classical, and it was all the better for the box-office.

When Elizabeth came to the throne in 1558, drama was one of the most popular amusements. But it was still primitive enough, though the man who was to be its greatest glory was born six years from her accession. The various forms were developing more definite characteristics of their own, and the classics were colouring them all. Secular drama in the mid-century was poor stuff, but it was there, and with a keenly interested audience to be ready for the great developments of the fifteen-eighties.

Just about the time of Elizabeth's accession and the birth of the dramatist who was her greatest subject, there come a quartet of famous plays, which are worth a little individual description as the seeds of what was to flower in twenty years. They show for the first time that English had achieved real tragedy, real comedy, and real historical drama, and that the farce already extant in the interludes had developed till it could be the substance of a play.

King Johan, the history, shows very closely its connection with the older forms: indeed, Bishop Bale, who wrote it, was born within the fifteenth century, and had written several moralities. It is in fact not very far removed from them, for many of the characters are still personified abstractions. But the point of the mention here is that many of them are not, for the lesson of it is to be conveyed through the showing of an incident from secular history. It is not, to be sure, very historical history: King John's defiance of the Pope is such whelming virtue that it covers all his less attractive qualities. It is not even a lively specimen of the morality: but here for the first time we have real historical figures moving among the abstractions – not Kingship but a particular and specific king, a person, not a quality.

There is more real drama, by a good deal, in the two lively comedies, *Ralph Roister Doister* and *Gammer Gurton's Needle*. Here the descent is through the interlude from the lively if rough-and-ready realistic interpolations in the mysteries. They are both plays of every-day life in an English village. But they are written by scholars, *Ralph* by Nicholas Udall, Headmaster of Eton in the reign of Mary, the *Gammer* probably by Bishop Still, who lived into the seventeenth century and the reign of James, dying in 1608, when Shakespeare's work was very nearly over. Being scholars' plays, they show beneath them the new modes of the Renaissance, and there is nearly as much of Plautus in them as of the interludes. *Ralph Roister Doister* has a quite elaborate plot, of the hero's suit to a fair and wealthy widow. Ralph is the traditional boastful coward of both Latin comedy and the mediæval mysteries – the type that grew into Parolles and Bobadil and Bob Acres: and it is significant that much of the fun depends, however crudely, upon character, not merely incident. It is quite funny, too, in a rough-and-tumble sort of fashion, with the dialogue in a robustious swinging doggrel whose effect is not unlike the Plautian septenarius. *Gammer Gurton's Needle*, though some fifteen years later,[1] is less elaborate in plot, but vigorous enough, and the vituperative dialogue – the loss of the needle devastates a whole village, till it turns up again in Hodge's breeches – has a considerable, if not very episcopal, brio.

Gorboduc, printed in 1561, three years before Shakespeare's birth, is on its merits much the least interesting: it is duller even than *King Johan*. To the student of the development of the theatre, however, it is interesting enough, though he would be a bold man who attempted to produce it. Yet it is very notably a landmark, since here for the first time in English you have serious drama for its own sake, drama not *primarily* didactic in its intention, though it has a moral, which is well rubbed in. And what is equally significant, it takes the English language seriously enough to attempt in it what the great Greeks had done in theirs. It was the work of two men of letters, Thomas Norton, not otherwise remarkable, and Thomas Sackville, Lord Buckhurst, who in another place [2] wrote poetry of a sombre, almost grim magnificence.

Gorboduc, however, is work of the scholar's intelligence rather than the poet's imagination. It has, at the same time, initiative. For the first time we have in English a five-act tragedy in blank verse – the typical Elizabethan form that was to come. In handling, however, it does not greatly resemble its successors, for it is on strictly classical lines, more Greek than Senecan, for the Roman, to the delight of his Elizabethan followers, had no compunction about the representation before the audience of such violent action as Medea's murder of her children, while Sackville and Norton, following

---

[1] Its date and authorship are neither of them quite certain. But it was played at Cambridge in 1566, when Shakespeare was a baby.

[2] The Induction to a series of tales called *The Mirror for Magistrates*

Greek convention, have their action, violent in itself, described by messengers. As a quaint enough concession to popular taste, however, the Messenger's speeches are supplemented by interludary 'dumbshows,' which show in pantomime what is to come. The device came to be used fairly often, and Shakespeare shows it as prelude to *The Murder of Gonzago*, which in both style and dramatic construction is a recollection of the literary drama of his own boyhood.

Structurally, *Gorboduc* has even more than the classic symmetry and balance. Gorboduc the King has two sons, Ferrex and Porrex, who have each a Counsellor and a Parasite. There are two Messengers, four Dukes, the King's secretary and counsellor, and four Ancients of Britain, who form the Chorus. It has long been a favourite professorial joke that one is almost surprised to find only one Queen. There is no action, and there is a great deal of moralizing, in speeches of enormous length. There is little life in it, as a whole or in parts: it has neither dramatic nor poetic quality. But at the same time it made an innovation that was to enrich both in its successors. It is the first English play to use as its medium the ten-syllabled iambic line, unrhymed, that by another quarter-century was to take on 'the thunder of the trumpets of the night,' in the hands of Marlowe, and in another the soaring flame of Cleopatra's mourning.

From *Gorboduc* to the middle of the fifteen-eighties, drama was popular, but one gathers that not much actual advance was made, as far as the plays themselves were concerned. There was an advance, though, and a great one. For the first time in England there was not only a drama but a theatre.

It was the Puritans who achieved it – an irony of fortune,

since they hated the drama as much as they hated 'that emblem of Satan, the crucifix.'[1] It may not have been all to the good, in the long run, that as they drove religion into one day of the week, so they drove drama into a special building: but at least by doing so they helped, for the time, its acquirement of an independent being. By forbidding dramatic representations within the jurisdiction of the City Fathers, they sent them across the river, or to such places as Shoreditch or Finsbury, where there were no buildings as suitable as the halls or galleried inn-yards where they had previously been given, so that the actors now were forced to build. In 1576 Richard Burbage, who ten years later was to be Shakespeare's manager, built *The Theatre*, which gave its name generically to its imitators, though for a long time *playhouse* is the commoner word. It was followed very soon by the *Curtain* at Shoreditch, the *Rose* at Southwark, the *Fortune*, the *Swan*, and most famous of them all, the Southwark *Globe*, Burbage's again, in which Shakespeare, by then a well-known and successful dramatist, was a shareholder.

Of the detail of them we know really very little more than of the many plays of their first decade, which survive as names or are entirely lost. We gather that they were large galleried buildings, oval or circular, unroofed save for the surrounding galleries and the rectangular stage which projected in front of that part of the circle where were the dressing-rooms and so forth. The wealthier part of the audience sat for the most

---

[1] The ecclesiastical origin and associations of the drama may have had something to do with it, of course. But as Puritan metaphysics, and consequently Puritan ethics, were essentially manichæan (see p. 28) all of the arts, with the curious exception of music, were considered to be obnoxious to the Creator. One wonders how much the German origin of the Reformation had to do with both the prohibitions and the exception.

part in the galleries. The dashing young sparks, who came to be seen rather than to see, achieved that end by having stools on the stage itself. The poorer section, long-suffering then as now, stood in the roofless pit, and did what they chose about the British climate, consoling themselves by a free expression of opinion.

The deep square stage thrust out towards the centre, so that the action was visible from three sides at once. It was entered by two doors at the back, and as there was no curtain to cut it off there could be no display of a number of characters already grouped to form a picture. A court, for instance – say *Hamlet*, I, ii – must enter in procession, and no doubt the entry could be used to give a sense of movement and pageantry that helped to make up for the deprivation of the revealed tableau. The stately withdrawal at the end of a tragedy, at all events, can make a most impressive close. The revealed group, too, was possible to some small extent, as the rearward portion of the stage, recessed between the entrances, was screened by a movable curtain called a traverse, behind which Polonius could eavesdrop, Florizel and his princess be revealed, or which might form Lear's or Desdemona's bed, the cave in *Cymbeline*, or Juliet's tomb. Above the recess or rear stage ran a gallery, which might hold spectators or musicians, or could be used also in the play itself, for Juliet's balcony, the walls of Angers in *King John*, or the windows whence Jessica elopes or Brabantio talks to Roderigo.

On the open stage there could be no scenery. It is supposed that a placard was hung out to denote the place – Rome, London, or Illyria. But the place is often very vaguely localized: those scenes that our editors describe as 'A street' or 'Another room in the palace,' are simply 'Anywhere.' If the setting is really significant, as the Blasted Heath or the dawn of the Ides of March, it comes as it were in solution – the scene-painting is in the speeches.

There were such necessary properties as chairs and tables, the well in *The Old Wife's Tale*, trapdoors leading below the stage, and so forth: but we do not know whether the movables were carried on in view of the audience or confined to the rear stage, where their changing could be hidden by the traverse. In the small semi-private theatres, which were roofed, and at court performances, there was artificial light, sometimes on a lavish scale, and there could thus be a certain amount of manipulation of it, though not very much, as of course it was confined to lamps and candles. In the roofless public theatres there was daylight. In the smaller ones again, there grew up later more elaborate machinery, and many of the court masques indeed had some such device for one of their main attractions.

But in the main, the staging was fairly primitive. What mattered was the thing done and the thing said

CHAPTER THREE

SHAKESPEARE'S SENIORS. I

THE UNIVERSITY WITS: COMEDY. LYLY. PEELE. GREENE

'Shaping fantasies.'

WILLIAM SHAKESPEARE, *Midsummer Night's Dream.*

✶

IN 1580 the Elizabethan drama was still but half-developed
as an art-form. In 1590 it was in being as a form very definite
indeed, and had produced plays that were not merely interesting to the student of dramatic history, but great literature and
– though less often and less certainly – great drama. The men
who did most to bring this change about were a group of
young scholars known as the University Wits. All of them
were men of talent, and all had flashes – in one case a good
deal more than that – of genius: and all but one of them died
under forty. Their names and approximate dates are John
Lyly (1554?–1606?), George Peele (1558?–1597?), Robert
Greene (1560?–1592), Christopher Marlowe (1564–1593)
and Thomas Kyd (1568?–   ?). Three of them were thus a
little older than Shakespeare, Marlowe his age, Kyd actually
younger. But they were his schoolmasters, for they all wrote
early, and his work begins rather unusually late: by the time
Marlowe's career was over (and Marlowe's last plays show
his power decaying) Shakespeare had written only some comparatively minor work, and half of that was in collaboration.

The dramatic chronology of the whole period is rather
obscure. In Shakespeare's case, patient research has set the
thirty-seven plays of the Second Folio into a fairly probable

38

sort of order: but even with him the arrangement of the earliest group is largely guess-work. A great number of plays, too, vanished completely. The custom of publishing playbooks for the reader does not grow common until the later 'eighties, when the drama was definitely taking rank with literature, and the words of it could be separated off and stand by themselves as entertainment. It was popular literature then, and tended to be well read and worn out quickly: even of the 'collected works' of a popular dramatist like Shakespeare, few copies survive. Many plays never saw print at all, existing only in a jealously guarded MS. prompt copy, which of course wore out in time. Often the printed ones appeared by no good will of either manager or author: an enterprising publisher would send a shorthand reporter to the theatre, or procure by bribes some hurried and surreptitious transcript of an actor's part, possibly supplemented from memory. Even the date of publication often tells little enough, especially as we seldom know for certain that an earlier edition is not lost to us. Some of Shakespeare's plays never, so far as we know, saw print until he had been seven years dead. The most we can really say with certainty, as a rule, is that at least the play must have been written *some time* before our earliest printed text of it.

The work of the Wits, then, cannot be exactly dated It does not matter very much: we know that they come more or less in the late 'eighties, and that when Shakespeare began to write they were 'the new men.' Each brought his own special and personal contribution to the thing they were bringing into life between them. LYLY, the eldest, had done much already for English prose, in his long narrative of *Euphues*, whose publication within a few months of Spenser's *Shep-*

heardes Kalendar makes 1579 the year from which we count
the great age of Elizabethan letters. *Euphues* brought him
name and fame at once. Its delicately balanced antithetic
sentences set the fashion of polite prose for the next decade –
not only written prose, but speech as well, for the court
beauty who could not 'parley Euphues' was as lacking in
accomplishment as though she could not dance. The temper
of the man shows through all his work. He was no rackety
Bohemian like the rest, but a spruce courtier, whose dominant
mood is glittering, rather melancholy satire. Prose is his
natural medium, though his lyric verse is sometimes exquisite, as in the universally known

> 'Cupid and my Campaspe played
> At cards for kisses. Cupid paid. . . .'

He belongs to the tradition of the masque rather than the
main stream of Elizabethan drama, for all his eight plays[1]
were written for court performance, not by professional
players but by 'The Children of the Chapel Royal' or 'of
Paul's' – that is, the choristers. They have a strong family
likeness to each other, but are not at all like those of the
other 'Wits,' except for the usual flavour of the classics. But
Lyly's object is not so much to show human beings perform-
ing more or less interesting actions, still less to show human
character and emotion revealed in action – a purpose which
had to wait for Marlowe to begin and Shakespeare to perfect.
What he wanted was to supply a court entertainment, in the
height of intellectual fashion, and with a certain topical

---

[1] *The Woman in the Moon, Campaspe, Sappho and Phao, Endymion,
Galatea, Midas, Mother Bombie, Love's Metamorphosis,* and a doubtful
ninth, *The Maid's Metamorphosis.*

point, discreetly veiled. His general method is to take a classical myth, with a 'love interest' or the possibility of inserting one, to infuse a strong element of the courtly artificial pastoral, such as was very popular on the Continent, and to colour the whole with the topical satire that pastoral so often held. The whole could slip easily into an allegoric veil for current events: in *Endymion*, for instance, Cynthia, Lady of the Moon, is not only type of regnant Chastity but a thin disguisal of the Maiden Queen, and her platonic love for Endymion glances politely at that lady's philanderings with Leicester.[1] The loves of the hero or heroine are helped or hindered by a medley of assorted personages – gods and goddesses, nymphs and shepherds, Renaissance-classic philosophers and completely English fairies, with a crowd of pages and waiting-women who have been drawn with one eye on Plautus, one on London, and whose quick repartee provides a foil for the more courtly and sentimental wit of the main characters, while their pranks make a politer substitute for the old buffoonery of Vice and Devil that had been the 'comic relief' of the popular mysteries. The human interest, as a rule, is shadowy, though one can see in it the beginnings of Romantic Comedy, that later became *Twelfth Night* and *As You Like It*. The main point dramatically, apart from the spectacular one of splendid costume, music, and graceful movement, is the dialogue, which in all but *The Woman in the Moon*, his first play, is polished prose, lit with a brilliant, rather chilly fancy and a satire with more melancholy than wrath in it. It is the prose that his own *Euphues* had already made the dialect of the Court:

[1] The same sort of topicalism shows in – and does not improve – the *Faerie Queene*. Some very clever people have tried to discover a much more acute form of it in *Hamlet* and *Othello*.

'O fair Cynthia, why do others term thee inconstant, whom I have ever found unmovable? Injurious time, corrupt manners, unkind men, who finding a constancy not to be matched in my sweet mistress, have christened her with the name of wavering, waxing and waning! Is she inconstant that keepeth a settled course, which since her first creation altereth not one minute in her moving? There is nothing thought more admirable or more commendable in the sea, than the ebbing and flowing; and shall the Moon, from whom the sea taketh his virtue, be accounted fickle for increasing and decreasing? Flowers in their buds are nothing worth till they be blown; nor blossoms accounted till they be ripe fruit; and shall we say that they be changeable for that they grow from seeds to leaves, from leaves to buds, from buds to their perfection? Then, why not twigs that become trees, children that become men, and mornings that grow to evenings, termed wavering, for that they continue not at one stay?'

Suppled and humanized, in a key more spoken, less declamatory, the memory of its cadence is in the vivid lovely prose of Shakespeare, master of that as of 'the other harmony.' In Lyly himself there is something too much, perhaps, of buckram in it – it is not only stiff, but thin as well: yet it has at its best a stately formal wit and a pallid beauty, like the pale-coloured French paste set in fine silver that you find in jewel-boxes of the eighteenth century. And the lively rattle of his serving-men was the evident model for Shakespeare's comic characters.

It is true that Lyly's work has little in it properly dramatic: yet English drama is deeply in his debt. He helped very much to give it grace and lightness, to supply to comedy an intellectual element that lifts it above the level of mere farce: and he is the father of all English plays whose primary interest is in their dialogue – of Congreve and Sheridan, Wilde and Mr. Shaw and Harold Chapin. And he was one of Shakespeare's two great masters.

GEORGE PEELE, apparently a few years Lyly's junior – he was probably born in the year of the Queen's accession – is much more typical of the group generally. He was no serious fastidious courtier, but a professional (and disreputable) man of letters, though like Lyly's his dramatic work was for the courtier rather than the citizen. His plays have not the strong family likeness perceptible in those of Lyly: indeed the fantastic variety of their form and content has itself a reminiscence of the masque in it.

Like the others he had an eye to the classics, beginning indeed with a translation from Euripides. His earliest original play, at the beginning of the fifteen-nineties, is *The Arraignment of Paris* – a court entertainment on very much the lines of Lyly's, and like them meant to be acted by the Queen's choristers. It is again in the key of classico-allegorical compliment to the Queen, but Peele prefers, instead of prose, the verse more normally the dramatic medium of the time, though he does not stick to blanks, using in fact, like Greene and the young Shakespeare, a lot of couplet, and even occasionally the long 'fourteener.' *Sir Clyomon and Sir Clamydes*, an odd thing, is all in the fourteener, and reverts to the Middle Ages not only in theme but in the appearance of some allegoric personages and the comic 'Vice' of the moralities: but it is possibly not Peele's at all. *Edward I* mixes prose, blank verse, and rhyme, *The Old Wife's Tale* prose and blank verse, while in *The Battle of Alcazar* and *David and Bethsabe* he has settled into blank verse only, and often very beautiful verse, for all its stiffness. Marlowe is by far the greatest poet of the group, but Peele was a real one: and it is probably their joint influence that established the ten-syllabled unrhymed iambic as the regular medium for serious drama.

Peele was a better hand at comedy than tragedy, and more a poet than a dramatist. *Edward I* and *The Battle of Alcazar* are loose-hung stuff, high-coloured with wild rant – the sort of thing that Ancient Pistol loved. The latter is meant to catch the popular anti-Spanish feeling, and no doubt did. *David and Bethsabe* is a good deal better than either. It dramatizes, loosely but with a certain point and coherence, the story of Absalom's revolt against his father, out of revenge for Amnon's unpunished rape of their sister Tamar, which wars are seen as Heaven's punishment for the King's treachery against Uriah. In theme it thus suggests the miracles, but the treatment is that of the 'history' or chronicle-play, like *Henry VI*. It has coherence and a stiff-jointed dignity: the logic of events is clearly seen in it. But the interest in the main is purely in event, and not in the character that causes or the emotions that are caused by it. It has poetry, though: there are many places where the verse, stiff yet, in the old single-moulded form, rises to beauty, as in David's praises of Bethsabe when first he sees her:

> 'May that sweet plain that bears her pleasant weight
> Be still enamelled with discoloured flowers;
> That precious fount bear sand of purest gold;
> And for the pebble, let the silver streams
> That pierce Earth's bowels to maintain the source
> Play upon rubies, sapphires, chrysolites;
> The brim let be embraced with golden curls
> Of moss that sleeps with sound the waters make
> For joy to feed the fount with their recourse . . .'

The Arraignment of Paris is the tale of the golden apple, and Paris' luckless choice between the goddesses. It is court masque, and dramatically empty, but has some really lovely verse about it.

But the best of Peele's work, to a modern, is *The Old Wife's Tale*, which is the quaintest and most charming farrago of elements, that shift with the inconsequence of dream. One can scarcely call it a play, and it is not a masque in the ordinary sense of the word: though it probably gave Milton the idea for *Comus*, there is no more resemblance than between a Della Robbia plaque of impish boy-faces and the serenity of the Elgin Marbles: perhaps 'revue' would be the best word for it. And with all its inconsequence, it stages pleasantly. Three travellers, Antic, Frolic, and Fantastic, come to the house of the Old Wife, who gives them a night's lodging, and begins to tell the tale, when the whole thing shifts to dreamland, comes alive, and acts itself. It is the tale of a lady taken captive by a wicked enchanter and released, but here is no frame of Greek myth and Platonic ethic. The tale itself is strewn with folk-lore marvels, 'authorized by our grandam.' Instead of a seriously pagan Comus, the wizard Sacrapant is first cousin to a pantomime Wicked Uncle. The whole blends the romance of Grimm with the broad folk-comedy of Robin Goodfellow, laced with a memory or two of Apuleius, and scattered with impish parody of the ranting Senecan drama, as in the giant with the nice robustious name Huanebango, and with scraps of country song like

> 'All ye that lovely lovers be
>   Pray you for me.
> Lo here we come a-sowing, a-sowing,
>   And sow sweet fruits of love.
> In your sweet hearts well may it prove.'

GREENE'S work, like Peele's, is best in comedy. He was less of a poet than Peele, but rather more of a dramatist, and helped more than any of them to found the type of romantic comedy that Shakespeare took up in *The Two Gentlemen of Verona* and made later into *Twelfth Night* and *Much Ado.* He has rather more interest in personality than the others, or at all events his plays show more of it. There is no great power of analysing character, but in one play at least his people are people, as Peele's are not.

Greene wrote a good deal, but comparatively little of what has survived of it is drama. He is one of the candidates for *Fair Em,* which has also been ascribed, on grounds dubious enough, to Shakespeare: but his best plays are two romantic comedies, *Friar Bacon and Friar Bungay* and *James IV.* Both are chaotic – the latter very much so. But *Friar Bacon,* at least, has continuity if not much unity, and also a good deal of charm. It even acts pleasantly enough if you are content to take it as it comes and not expect it to be what it is not. There is something of the spirit of *The Old Wife's Tale* in it, or the old songs like *The Bailiff's Daughter of Islington.* Lacy, sent to court a country girl for his master the Prince of Wales, falls honourably in love with her, and she with him. For a while they are in danger, but the Prince is a good fellow at heart and repents his anger, so it all ends happily. Mixed up with it is the magic of the great enchanter Bacon and his burlesque rival Friar Bungay – folk-lore magic, as the loves of Lacy and Margaret are folk romance. The whole is a pleasant straightforward affair, and Margaret herself, oddly the most living figure in it, recovers some of the charm of Chaucer's ladies, Custance and Candace and 'Emilye the shene.' One can see in her a foreshadowing of Shakespeare's heroines of comedy. Greene is careful, too, that spectacle is not forgotten: we have a coronation, the bringing home of a royal bride, and such incidents of Bacon's conjuring as a vision of Hercules plucking the golden apples in spite of a property dragon who spits fire.

James IV is very much inferior. *Friar Bacon*, played to-day, would have a certain intrinsic charm as well as curiosity: *James IV* would be curio and nothing more. That it most certainly is, and nowhere more than in its choice of title. The plot is a Grimm's Fairy-tale, without the magic. Under the temptations of Ateukin, who is simply the Vice of the Morality, King James falls in love with the fair Ida, and as nothing less than marriage will have any chance with the lady, determines to murder his virtuous queen Dorothea, who escapes, and after various adventures in man's clothes, returns in time to save her now penitent husband from the vengeance of her father, while Ida is happily married to her Eustace. The whole is oddly framed in a queer induction. Bohan, an old Scots hermit, is disturbed by Oberon and his elves, and defends his retreat from the world by conjuring up a pageant of its frailties, in which his own three sons, two good and one villanous, play part – the events of the plot, to which are added, with no smallest attempt at relevance, all sorts of interludes, from an elaborate dumbshow of Semiramis to a jig by the aforesaid knavish son Slipper. The setting is nearly as odd as the garnish. There is nothing in itself remarkable in the choice of Scotland, any more than France or Venice or Illyria, for the Englishman has always loved a touch of the exotic to give his art prestige: even the charming Madame Butsova would have had a much harder fight as Miss Hilda Boot. But the selection of that particular king is most remarkable, for the real James had in fact been the husband of an English princess, aunt to Greene's sovereign, and the end of his reign was well within Greene's own century. Dorothea, to be sure, is English, but it is her sole resemblance to bustling much-married Margaret Tudor. She has charm, though, and a faint touch of personality: indeed, she is the nearest thing to a person in the play. In spite of the rather flagrant unhistoricity, there is a certain attempt at local colour in the speeches of Bohan in the interludes – though Greene's Scots, certainly, is rather wonderful. But during the play itself this concession to accuracy is abandoned.

CHAPTER FOUR

SHAKESPEARE'S SENIORS. II

THE UNIVERSITY WITS: TRAGEDY. KYD. MARLOWE. SHAKESPEARE'S BEGINNINGS

'The world being in proportion inferior to the soul.'
FRANCIS BACON, *The Advancement of Learning.*

★

THE tragedians of the group are the better playwrights. *Edward II* is a really great play: *The Spanish Tragedy*, if hardly that, stages effectively at any rate.[1] Neither Kyd nor Marlowe has much interest in character as such, but at their best they live so intently in the action and experience they are portraying that we find ourselves faced with real and strong emotions. Marlowe, to the back of that, was a poet, and a very great one. Peele, even Greene, gives music often to the decasyllable: Marlowe puts flame and ring of trumpets into it. Also, like none of the others, and very few men at any time, he can base a play on some intense conception, that dominates and fires it into unity.

Of KYD's work, the remains are very scanty. There is in fact only one certain play of his: but that is notable in itself and was the most popular play of its generation. We can see its effect, directly enough, in *Hamlet*, and it is probable that it was Kyd himself who in 1594 produced an older *Hamlet*, now lost, from which Shakespeare apparently lifted the plot of his own. The success of *The Spanish Tragedy* brought out a

---

[1] Like *The Old Wife's Tale, Friar Bacon*, and *Edward II* it was played recently at Birkbeck College. I cannot resist adding that it was nearly censored, on grounds not of morality but of politics!

D

hastily botched-up *First Part of Jeronimo* a few weeks later, purporting to show the events before the beginning of the other. But even if Kyd wrote it, it is only a hurried pot-boiler. What he survives by is *The Spanish Tragedy*.

That, and anything else that we know of him, shows Kyd to be a whole-souled Senecan. Murder and vengeance, vengeful ghosts and rant – I find my own pen slipping into bombastic blank verse when I come to write about him! Indeed, he was even in his own day rather a byword for Grand Guignol effects, and of course the nineteenth-century professors all poked fun at him. A joke about Kyd used to be a pretty safe ornament for an examination-paper. But the Grand Guignol was very successful in twentieth-century London; and personally I prefer Kyd. After all, he has only one corpse above the casualty-list of *Hamlet*, whose concluding quartet of them is directly in Kyd's tradition – and in the tradition, also, of some contemporary very actual history. It is true that Kyd is rather too content with the horrors merely *as* horrors. Yet he has imagination, too: there is both terror and pity in the play, though it is fair to add that the scenes which show most of them are not Kyd's own but a later addition of Ben Jonson's, who gets into Hieronimo's dialogue with the Painter more than a touch of the nightmare-and-storm effect that Webster later was to use magnificently.

The play opens with an induction relating it to the favourite motif of the Senecan drama – a dead man's claim for vengeance. The ghost of the Spaniard Andrea, slain in battle, enters with Revenge, who prophesies retribution on his slayer, the Portuguese Don Balthasar. Balthasar is sent prisoner to Spain, and falls in love with the King's niece, the Duke of Castile's daughter Bellimperia, who had been formerly betrothed to the dead Andrea. Her love is won by

Balthasar's captor and the dead man's friend, Horatio, son to Hieronimo, Marshal of Spain: but Balthasar and her brother murder him before her eyes. His father, maddened, seeks vengeance, and wins it at last, with Bellimperia's help, in a play performed before the Court, where the dramatic murders are made real ones, and the whole ends with a lurid forecast from the Ghost of the fate of his enemies in the next world.

There is rant, and lots of it; and in the Ghost especially, a naive and crude insistence on the horrors. But there is real drama, too. The play marches: it has momentum, which is one of the most precious of gifts in a story-teller, narrative or dramatic. Things happen rapidly and vividly, and what is more, coherently, with a wild logic in them. It plays, in fact, extremely well: I have seen it, and it was most effective. Indeed, it probably stages better than some things that are much greater literature. And – though again the passage is probably not Kyd's – one cannot deny a very real dramatic quality to dialogue like that in which Hieronimo reveals his knowledge of his son's death to Lorenzo who has murdered him, and whom, as the King's nephew, he cannot strike. Hieronimo enters, seeking Bellimperia, Lorenzo's sister and the dead man's lover, who is to share the vengeance he is planning. Lorenzo meets him, and offers to carry her a message.

Hier. Nay, nay, my lord, I thank you: it shall not need.
    I had a suit unto her, but too late.
    And her disgrace makes me unfortunate.
 Lor. Why so, Hieronimo? Use me.
Hier. Who? You, my lord?
    I reserve your favour for a greater honour.
    This is a very toy, my lord, a toy

Lor. All's one, Hieronimo. Acquaint me with it.
Hier. I' faith, my lord, it is an idle thing.
     I must confess I ha' been too slack, too tardy,
     Too remiss unto your honour.
Lor. How now, Hieronimo?
Hier. In troth, my lord, it is a thing of nothing:
     The murder of a son, or so . . .
     A thing of nothing, my lord.

The sheer flare of hate in the last words is rather withering. And if a good many other speeches are rant, it is a rant with genuine emotion in it.

The Spanish Tragedy, notable in itself, is even more so from the historic standpoint, for its immense success gave it a powerful influence even on dramatists who frankly sneered at it. The balanced rhetoric of the style –

   'O eyes, no eyes but fountains fraught with tears!
   O life, no life, but lively form of death!' –

caught the ear, both seriously and in parody. The strange ironic effect of the play within the play – a mirror showing in another, reflecting the wild issues of the action – recurs again: *Hamlet* is one of many instances. The ghost of a man wronged and murdered, watching the slow revenge of time upon his slayer, is a favourite effect that we find subtilized in *Julius Cæsar*, and in *Hamlet* and *Macbeth* given a newer and more complex function: while *Richard III* throughout has nearly as much of Kyd in its inspiration as Marlowe, notably in the ghost-chorus at the close. The gloomy gorgeous rhetoric at which Kyd was aiming, and which he does indeed sometimes achieve, charging it with a looming shadowed poetry, caught the ear of his age – as did the fustian when he

failed achievement, which bred innumerable tags and catch-
words. 'Go by, Jeronimy' is the Elizabethan for the 'Yes, we
have no bananas' that infested London a few years ago.

MARLOWE produced one play at least that is dramatically as
effective. Indeed, two more of his might conceivably be effective enough on the stage, given the (rather difficult) right conditions: and all these, and a fourth that is dramatically weak,
are coloured with a gorgeous poetry. Indeed, he is the king
of the whole group.

He was probably a year or two older than Kyd, and was
certainly born in the same year as Shakespeare. But as he
wrote early and Shakespeare began rather late, and as Marlowe, too, did his greatest work at the beginning, he is Shakespeare's senior professionally, and (with Kyd) was the greater
artist's master in tragedy, as Greene and still more Lyly were
in comedy. He was under thirty when he died in a Deptford
tavern on Ingram's dagger: but it is unlikely that we have
occasion to mourn his 'unfulfilled renown,' for his latest plays
have his faults with very little of his virtues. The four that
count – and they count superbly – are his earliest: the two
parts of *Tamburlaine the Great* (*c.* 1586) *Doctor Faustus,* and
Edward II. The Jew of Malta has the faults of these,
worsened and elaborated, but with here and there a flash of
the great poetry. *Dido Queen of Carthage* – perhaps not all
his – has some poetry to it too, but in the main is pretty
negligible. *The Massacre at Paris* shows, like Chapman's
chief plays, an incident of almost contemporary history,
material for effective melodrama, but reduced to a dull chronicle of horrors.

Dramatically – indeed in any way – Marlowe's touch is
not certain: but it is he, in *Edward II,* who first achieves the

clash and interplay of personalities that is essential drama. *Tamburlaine* and *Faustus* are related to this type rather as melody to harmony. There is no interplay of personality: but there is personality itself, in the great central figures who dominate each and are shown first in their huge impact on circumstance, and then in the reaction on themselves of that circumstance' inexorable law. They tower in the splendid verse that is filled with

> 'those brave translunary things
> That the first poets had. His raptures were
> All air and fire . . .'[1]

Tamburlaine and *Faustus* are not so much true plays as splendid dramatic lyrics. Yet in the former at all events the adjective counts equally with the noun. The double play is the tale of the Scythian shepherd who conquered the Eastern world, and is full of the trampling of armies, the downfall of great kings, 'the battle afar off, the thunder of the captains, and the shouting,' subdued and dominated by one vast shadowy figure who sweeps relentless on his path with kings and emperors drawing his chariot like beasts of burden. But human power and splendour are touched with the mortality of this 'momentous and nugatory gift of life,' and there is an enemy beyond his power: his queen Zenocrate is taken from him:

> 'The golden ball of heaven's eternal fire
> That danced with glory on the silver waves'

is darkened, and then he learns that a world-conqueror 'shall die like men and fall like one of the princes' – 'thy pomp is

---

[1] Drayton, *To Henry Reynolds, Of Poets and Poetry.*

gone down to the grave and the noise of thy viols,' and he dies also, calling at the last for a map and pointing to his sons those countries yet unconquered.

This towering shadow, the very eidolon of the Renaissance, is the play. All in its action is there to show his power and his desire. It does show those: the dramatic outline is simple, but it is adequate. We have more than one producer and designer who could stage it now. What we lack is actors who could speak its verse, and in another twenty years we may have found them, and hear again, *in its place*, the great speech upon beauty or the other that states what is – with Death's ironic commentary – the central theme of the whole flaming play:

> 'Nature, that framed us of four elements,
> Warring within our breasts for regiment,
> Doth teach us all to have aspiring minds.
> Our souls, whose faculties can comprehend
> The wondrous architecture of the world
> And measure every wandering planet's course,
> Still climbing after knowledge infinite
> And always moving as the restless spheres,
> Will us to wear ourselves, and never rest
> Until we reach the ripest fruit of all,
> That highest bliss and sole felicity,
> The sweet fruition of an earthly crown.'

Tamburlaine has a sort of symphonic unity, a balance and coherence of its parts, though it is probably true that it might be bettered dramatically by a cutting that should fuse both parts in one. (Yet audiences listen to *The Ring*.) *Faustus* is different stuff. There are parts as fine as anything in the other – passages of it indeed are perhaps even finer: but one is not surprised that the recent attempt to stage it proved unsatisfying, for though the beginning and the end are splendid, the middle is mostly crude and feeble farce – not Marlowe's, probably: the textual evidence goes to show that our version is the play as mangled by a manager, with heavy cuts and corresponding insertions. It is conceived as something of a parallel to the other. *Tamburlaine* is the Renaissance hunger for power – material, or rather temporal, power. *Faustus* is the Renaissance hunger for the knowledge that to an age drunk on the New Learning as our fathers were arrogantly drunk on the New Science, seemed the sole base of spiritual power. For knowledge and its power Faust sells his soul to Evil, and is brought face to face then with the awful ultimate 'what shall it profit a man?' His fall and his eventual fate make the play's greatness. Its weakness is that the use made of the power fails heavily to satisfy imagination: indeed, it is grossly trivial, save in the one great speech where he calls Helen's beauty from the shades, and cries

> 'Was this the face that launched a thousand ships
> And burnt the topless towers of Ilion? . .
> Sweet Helen, make me immortal with a kiss. –
> – Her lips suck forth my soul. See where it flies!
> Oh, thou art fairer than the evening air,
> Clad in the beauty of a thousand stars.'

There is drama enough, too, in scattered places, as in that grim dialogue with Mephistophilis where Faust asks of the lost angels, and in the tremendous close:

'Ah Faustus,
Now hast thou but one bare hour to live,
And then thou must be damned perpetually.

thing before Shakespeare found his feet. It is, simply, a great play, without any allowance for curiosity or mere student's interest. It is no intenser in its life than *Tamburlaine*, but it is wider, more harmonized and orchestrated. In each of its predecessors there is one great figure, launched on a course that can have but one end, whither it moves as if in a procession. In *Edward II* there is an ebb and flow, a clash of forces between Mortimer and the King, with the Queen aiding first her husband and then as her wrongs grow unbearable his enemy, rising with Mortimer to power on the King's ruin, and borne down with him in the crashing overthrow that comes in the very moment of his triumph. They are people, all of them, not merely vehicles for great emotions. The others – Warwick, Lancaster, and so on – are background, though some of them are by no means puppets: and Gaveston, the King's worthless favourite who is the chief occasion of the feuds, stands for the effeminate luxury that was one of the dooms of the Renaissance passion for the lust of the eye and the pride of life. The whole play, by the way, is utterly of the Renaissance: except in the sense that the basic human issues and passions are common to all ages, it is no more mediæval than yesterday's *Times*.

It is commonly said of *Edward II* that though the King's personality is wonderfully projected in the individual scenes, the character as a whole is not convincing – that the hysterica. weakling of the early acts is too dignified a victim at the endl In reading the play, indeed, this has some justice. But until 1920 no man for more than three centuries had seen it staged: the stage was what Marlowe wrote for, and on the stage it is far more coherent. Edward, after all, is a king and a strong king's son, and it is easier to be dignified in disaster than in victory. A similar charge is brought against the

Queen, and to the *reader*, in fact, the change from long-suffering devotion to rancorous hatred does seem to come about a little suddenly. On the stage, however, we see her wrongs more evidently, and see also the growing influence of Mortimer, who offers her, at first in all honour, the protection she is very sorely needing. The King's unjust suspicions fix Mortimer in her imagination – and in a while Mortimer's powerful will has made them true. On the stage, indeed, the relations of the three are entirely convincing: seeing them in sixteenth-century dress, as Marlowe saw them, I was made more than once to wonder how far their creator had in his mind Bothwell, Mary of Scots, and Darnley.

The real dramatic flaw in the play, and in point of fact a rather serious one, is not in character-drawing but that in mid-passage of the action our sympathies are forced abruptly to change sides. For half of it, King Edward is the villain of the piece, and all our regard is for the Queen and barons: in the second half we are invited instead to sympathize with Edward, and reprobate Lord Mortimer and the Queen. But though this breach of emotional unity flaws the play somewhat as a whole, it does not spoil the individual scenes of it. They, in their own place on the stage, are superbly dramatic, even those that in the printed volume read confusedly. Touches, too, like the Queen's check of Mortimer's flaring arrogance, that teaches her to realize her power on him, or the sense of foreboding over the King's capture, have an extraordinary life in them. There is nothing that stands poetically with the great purple patches of the earlier plays, yet many of the speeches are magnificent, and again and again we have lines like Mortimer's defiance of his fall:

'Base Fortune, now I see that in thy wheel
There is a point to which when men aspire
They tumble headlong down. That point I reached,
And seeing there was no place to mount up higher,
Why should I grieve at my declining fall?
Farewell, fair queen. Weep not for Mortimer,
That scorns the world, and as a traveller,
Goes to discover countries yet unknown.'

It is sometimes said by people irritated by the Shakespear-olaters that Marlowe, had he lived, would have been a greater dramatist than Shakespeare. It is not true. Marlowe had great conceptions, but the greatness is of reach, not depth: he draws in superb bold strokes, but without subtlety. He had comparatively little sense of structure – though much more, all the same, than he gets credit for: and he had no sense of humour, and therefore no reliable self-criticism. But he was the first to prove that English drama could handle a great theme greatly, and did more than anyone to fashion the verse that was its medium for a mighty generation. It is a fairly considerable achievement for a man who died at twenty-nine: and we *can* say, with perfect justice, that if Shakespeare had died then too – and he was Marlowe's age – Marlowe would then have been the greater, unless perhaps by *Romeo and Juliet*. And even that, as lovely as it is, has less of substance, though it shows (now that we know what followed) the promise of more than Marlowe could aspire to.

To end this group, though he is a pupil rather than, at any time, a member of it, comes the first work of Shakespeare, when he began in the late fifteen-eighties, at the time of the great deliverance from Spain. I am not set here on a detailed finger in the Second, and it is probable enough that he made the Third, rough as it is, from *The True Tragedy of Richard Duke of York*, which may have been a pot-boiler of Marlowe's. But it was in comedy that he was more at home then. He experimented there in several manners, but with more originality than in the tragedies. *The Taming of the Shrew* may be an old farce rewritten, though it is not improbable that *The Taming of a Shrew*, its reputed source, is merely a garbled version of itself. *The Comedy of Errors* is an experiment – perhaps with a memory of *Ralph Roister Doister* – in giving farce the unity and tight elaborate structure of the classics. *Love's Labour's Lost* is a court-comedy in the key of Lyly: the point of it dramatically is in the dialogue and the taking off of intellectual fashions, the various poses of the contemporary highbrow, with as more serious thread, a comedian's presentation of current theory on the relation of the sexes, that made it an Elizabethan *Man and Superman*. Most original of these eight 'prentice-works is *The Two Gentlemen of Verona*, where he follows Greene into romantic comedy, taking a subject from Spanish fiction and making much more of a play of it than Greene could – as Greene, by the way, knew very well and most indignantly. None of them matter very much, though all of them except *Titus* and *Henry VI Part One* are playable. He found his dramatic feet somewhere about the opening of the nineties, with *Midsummer Night's Dream* and *Romeo and Juliet*. The former belongs really to the masque, and like most masques, seems written for an 'occasion.' It has Lyly's combination of poetry, whimsical comedy, fairyland, and a dash of the classics, with a relief to them of low-life humours: but the elements are blended by a man who is not only a finer poet and a creator, as Lyly was not, of living characters, but who had a keen sense of the stage, and more than that, already that power of *structure* which, after, he had superbly almost always, in a degree that none of his contemporaries achieve – the power of presenting a body of complex events in a lucid and logically patterned action, co-ordinated and adequately concise, that reveals their significance. Indeed, this play is a remarkable piece of carpentry, in the dexterous structure that makes clear and shapely its complicated fourfold plot. *Romeo and Juliet* has not only this and even more of the poetry, but its characters are always living people, handled with subtle insight here and there, and an amazing vivid life throughout.

After it, he went back to the chronicle-tragedy. He had evidently been thinking hard about it, for though *King John* is no more than a refashioning – lively and vigorous, though – of an older play, the two *Richards* are obviously experiments in the application of two different methods. In *Richard III* he is following on Marlowe. The whole dramatic point of view on the subject is Marlowesque, with one powerful figure gripping the whole action, and there are echoes too of Marlowe in the writing. There is more humanity in the general run of the characters, but it seems half accidental, as if Shakespeare could not help feeling their point of view as well as his own playwright's and his hero's. A more important difference is that to Marlowe's dramatic qualities – save in parts of *Romeo and Juliet* he was not until later the *poetic* peer of Marlowe at his best – he adds a very carefully worked-out structure, as symmetrical as that of *The Comedy of Errors*, and like it with an apparent recollection of the classics, though the immediate basis may probably be a nearer recollection of *The Spanish Tragedy*, with its nemesis-revenges and its ghost.

In *Richard II* he is striking out more individually. The subject is one closely parallel to *Edward II*, which makes the difference from Marlowe more conspicuous. Here for the first time we have a play where the central point is the elaborate analysis of a character. It is not quite successful. Richard is wonderfully understood, but Shakespeare's concern is so absorbed by the hero in himself that he is as yet rather negligent of the action that should have revealed him: and also – perhaps deliberately – he tries to throw him into relief by flattening the rest into mere background, with the result that much of the play is at too low a temperature. But for all that, it is the first English play where the interest is primarily in the psychology – not the career – of an individual, so that although it is not among its writer's greatest work, it marks none the less a new epoch in the history of our drama.

NOTE.—There are many anonymous plays of about this time, though few of them have any notable merit. The best is *Arden of Feversham* (pub. 1592), a dramatization of a sixteenth-century Ilford Murder. It presents, baldly but with a good deal of force, the murder of a country gentleman by his wife and his low-born protégé Mosbie, her paramour. Interspersed with this are the humours of the comic ruffians. Black Will and Shakebag. It is crude to a degree (though it stages much better than it reads), its verse is wooden, and some of its serious scenes are almost farcical. Yet the man who wrote it had a real sense of the stage and a vivid if not a subtle imagination. Alice Arden, who dominates it, is a remarkable piece of work. The particular quality of her infatuation for the bounder Mosbie and her reaction to the accomplished murder are very well done, and give an actress splendid opportunities. Mosbie, his sister, and Michael are nearly as good if much less interesting. And if Arden's fascinated stupidity is improbable, no criminologist would have any difficulty in supplying a parallel from real life.

CHAPTER FIVE

SHAKESPEARE'S COMPANIONS. I

JONSON. CHAPMAN. MARSTON. *EASTWARD HO*

'Who have read the ancients with the greatest care.'
HARRY WOTTON, *Ancient and Modern Learning.*

*

CHRONOLOGICAL divisions in literature are always apt to be misleading, and this is never more the case than here. Nevertheless, if we are careful to remember that the groups all overlap in point of time, it is both possible and profitable to arrange the dramatists who come after Lyly into groups in whose work we can trace clearly the usual three stages of any artistic movement – a preliminary one of experiment and initiation, one of achievement, and a decadence when the new thing has caught the imagination of the little men, and made them imitate the externals of their betters.

> 'Hobbes hints blue. Straight he turtle eats.
> Nobbes prints blue. Claret crowns his cup.
> Nokes outdares Stokes in azure feats:
> Both gorge. Who fished the murex up?
> What porridge had John Keats?'

By the middle of the fifteen-nineties the first phase was over. The Wits had brought the drama into being: their greatest pupil, having tried his hand at Plautian comedy, romantic tragedy, tragedy of revenge, pure comedy of ideas, tragicomedy, and the popular chronicle-history, which might include elements from several of these, was settling down to a steady spell of work at the chronicle, with interludes of comedy, both which he was to bring by 1600 to the topmost

66

Scots blood that gave him an even more variegated career
than most of his contemporaries: I like to think of him
soldiering in Holland, coming out between the lines to challenge a Spanish enemy to single combat, killing his man, and
cannily and classically taking the *spolia opima* before he left
him. The passion for learning that did not lose hold of the
practical issues was then common in England also, as it is
coming to be again: but one can trace a national colour in the
dour dry pungency of his humour, and in a certain turn for
abstract thought, which though it gave him some of his
notable quality as a critic, was by no means entirely a virtue
in creative work. We have some interesting glimpses of his
chequered early life, but they do not tell us how he became a
playwright. We know, however, that in 1597 he was an
actor working for Henslowe, and Mere's famous diary in
1598 mentions dramatic work of his: so it would seem that
like Shakespeare he began as an actor and refurbisher of his
company's stock of manuscript plays. Most of his 'prentice-
work is lost, though we know that it included collaboration
with Dekker and Chettle in *Robert II King of Scots*, which
was presumably (though in view of *James IV* not certainly)
a chronicle, in *The Scottish Tragedy*, and in a dramatization
of a contemporary murder-case, *The Page of Plymouth*, belonging to a class once popular and apparently numerous, of
which only a few Elizabethan examples have survived, though
it is not many years since small touring companies used to
play a Victorian specimen, *The Murder in the Red Barn*.

Jonson's fame began, however, with *Every Man in His
Humour* in 1598, which led a new movement in the drama,
and was followed in the next year by a companion-piece,
Every Man out of His Humour. *Cynthia's Revels* in 1600
has a dash of Lyly in it, with the old and by this time habitual

compliment to the Maiden Queen, then a blushing damsel
of some seventy summers. But the flavour of satire that in
Lyly is not much more than a rub of garlic on the salad-bowl
here becomes open war, starting a quarrel in which *The
Poetaster*, in 1601, was his next campaign. Two slight and
insignificant comedies, both pretty dull, come beside these.
Sejanus that followed, itself a literary experiment in tragedy
on more strictly classical lines than had been customary, got
him into trouble on a charge of 'papistry' and treason: and
Eastward Ho, which he shared with Chapman and Marston,
came very far from endearing him to King James – indeed,
he nearly lost his ears over it. Then, though, his luck turned.
In 1605 he began a long and brilliant series of court masques,
a form in which he was a recognized proficient: and in the
next few years – contemporaneously, that is, with the later
of Shakespeare's great tragedies and the romantic comedies
in the new mode that followed them – are Jonson's greatest
plays, *Volpone* (1605), *The Silent Woman* (1609) and *The
Alchemist* (1610) followed by *Catiline*, a companion-piece to
Sejanus, in 1611, and in 1614 by the uproarious farce of
Bartholomew Fair. He lived and wrote for the best part of
another quarter-century, but these are his last notable works
in drama proper. Much of his later writings was lost in a
fire that destroyed his library. His adventures were not soon
ended: for many years he was King of the Mermaid Tavern
and Lord of Letters, but his pugnacity made his reign a
stormy one. He quarrelled with Inigo Jones, his collaborator
in the masques the Queen loved so, and lost court favour,
won it again, and died full of years and honours, to be buried
in the Abbey with 'O rare Ben Jonson!' for his epitaph.

It is not only in drama that he is famous. Out of his sinewy
prosaic stuff there flower at times the most enchanting lyrics,

that have the fragile loveliness of Herrick's: and his epigrams and occasional verse have an Horatian felicity. His famous prefatory verses to the First Folio Shakespeare are characteristic in their union of good sense and generous praise. It is not quite irrelevant, even here, to notice how the throwing forward to the eighteenth century shows in the predominance of 'occasional' subjects, in vocabulary, and in the tendency to write a couplet with a fixed cæsura and a break of both sound and sense at each couplet's end. More than any of his brethren he is a critic-dramatist, a man intensely interested in the abstract principles of his art, and a little inclined to parade his knowledge of them: he is as fond as Mr. Shaw of talking about his plays in an elaborate preface. Like Mr. Shaw, too, he enjoyed his difference from his fellows: one feels that if he had lived in the eighteenth century, when every one else was classical, rational, and realist, he would have found life dull. He has the eighteenth-century point of view not only in his reverence for antiquity – that is in all the Renaissance, though they show it differently – but in his avowed design 'to follow Nature,' by which, as usual, he means not the bundle of fantasies that Nature is, but whatever to himself seems natural – in this case the practice of great writers of antiquity. He is not, however, blindly a classicist, saying himself,

'Nothing is more ridiculous than to make an author a dictator, as the schools have done Aristotle. . . . Let Aristotle and others have their dues; but if we can make further discoveries of truth and fitness than they, why are we envied?'[1]

In the same way, he is a realist only in so far as he takes, in the words of one of his biographers, 'the actual rather than the splendid' – a phrase which begs the question rather neatly,

[1] *Discoveries.*

though Ben himself would probably acquiesce in the antithesis. But in fact 'reality' and 'realism' are two quite
different things: the one is an aim, the other a method, but
not the only method, of achieving it. It is only in the little
men that there is much genuine difference, at bottom, between 'realist' and 'romanticist': the one shirks facts, the
other is obsessed by them, and as neither can reach through
them to the truth, there is a certain unity even in them.

Jonson's great contribution to dramatic form is 'the comedy
of humours,' a phrase that may demand a moment's explanation for those who have been fortunate enough in the past
to avoid an evergreen examination question. To the physio-
logist of the Renaissance, as to Chaucer's Pertelote, a man's
physical and mental make-up was determined (in an antici-
pation of our gland-physiology), by the particular blend in
him of four liquids or 'humours,'[1] black bile, red bile
or choler, blood, and phlegm, which corresponded to the
four elements, earth, fire, air, water,[2] which were considered
the ultimate constituents of all matter whatsoever. The
mixture of these humours in the individual was his *temperament* (mixture) or *complexion* (folding together) or *disposition*
(arrangement): and when one humour was present to excess,
the mental qualities it produced were also excessive, and the
man was – as we still call him, in spite of a different physio-
psychology – sanguine, choleric, phlegmatic, or melancholy,
according to which one of them predominated. From this
use of the word, *humour* came to mean any idiosyncrasy which
markedly coloured a man's mind and temper, revealing itself
in external caprice or mannerism. That is what the word

---

[1] Latin (*h*)*umor-em*, moisture, cf. (*h*)*umidus*, our *humid*.
[2] Earth (cold and dry)=bile. Fire (hot and dry)=choler. Air (hot
and moist)=blood. Water (cold and moist)=phlegm.

chiefly meant to the Elizabethans. It is not till later that it
took on the modern sense, where it came to mean primarily
not a cause, but a quick and relishing observation, of the lack
of balance and proportion in the qualities of a man or an
event, as when we speak of 'a sense (perception) of humour' –
where the word is only just emerging from the old meaning –
or 'the humour of Jane Austen,' where *humour* alone is
practically equivalent to the whole phrase, 'sense of humour.'
To Jonson, what the word means is one of the foibles or
eccentricities of mankind, whose observation much delighted
him: a 'humorist' to him is what we should call a 'crank.'
He would have loved our semi-educated intellectuals, and
delights in the kind of person who nowadays believes that the
complete regeneration of the world is merely a matter of vege-
tarianism, psycho-analysis, folk-dancing, or prohibition, or
who is proud of standing for twenty hours in a Gaiety queue.

His comedy is essentially a portrayal of types, and suffers
therefore the inevitable danger of becoming a puppet-play of
dried stock figures, with as much resemblance to life as a
kipper has to a herring in its native water.[1] To some extent

---

[1] His own words show that he himself was not unaware of the danger.
He defines a 'humour':

> 'Some one peculiar quality
> Doth so possess a man, that it doth draw
> All his affects, his spirits and his powers,
> In their construction, all to run one way.'

But he adds as caution,

> 'But that a rook, by wearing a pied feather,
> The cable hatband, or the three-piled ruff,
> A yard of shoe-tie, or the Switzer's knot
> On his French garters, should affect a humour –
> Oh, it is more than most ridiculous.'
>   Prologue to *Every Man out of His Humour.*

his sheer vigour helps him to avoid this: his plays have a vivacity of idea and a vividness of drawing that give them life in spite of their lack of humanity. *Every Man in His Humour* held the stage until well on in the nineteenth century, and that although there is little in the way of plot or action: such as there is simply presents a gallery of types that strongly resemble those of Latin comedy – Kitely the jealous husband, Knowell the worried father, his graceless spark of a son, the elaborate cunning of the servant Brainworm, and Bobadil the braggart soldier with his oaths, 'By the foot of Pharaoh,' and so on – one of the most famous of all Jonson's characters. But for all their Latin source they have been coloured by Jonson's shrewd observation to fit completely in Elizabethan London – 'the London,' as Professor Herford puts it, 'of *Henry IV*, but handled with the method of *Love's Labour's Lost*.' Indeed, it is interesting to compare Bobadil and Falstaff, who both descend not only from the *miles gloriosus* of the Latin comedies, but from the braggart Herod of the mysteries. The comparison makes Jonson rather thin: but his play is a lively piece of the manners-painting to which the humour-comedy lends itself, since the 'humorist' or crank usually is one because he exaggerates something that has caught the popular imagination and is therefore colouring the social life. There is no point in a pose unless your audience can recognize it.

The play is ushered characteristically by a prologue which is something of a manifesto: he flings in the face of popularity, swears that his work is no pot-boiler, and tilts against the conventions of the stage, refusing

'To make a child, now swaddled, to proceed
Man, and then shoot up, in one beard and weed,

Past three-score years. . . .
He rather plays, you should be pleased to see,
One such, to-day, as other plays should be,'

with a concluding hope that 'You that have so graced monsters, may like men.' The bland assumption that he and he
only is virtuous was hardly likely to conciliate his brethren;
and it is the more amusing in that his own characters are no
more men than are the 'monsters' he is girding at. They are
some very lively and interesting things, certainly: but not
human beings. It would knock the play to pieces if they
were.

So much of a storm rose that he was discreet enough to
return to romantic comedy with *The Case is Altered,* a very
dull play with a very elaborate plot. It was not his vein, and
he knew it, for he would not include the play in the folio of
his collected works.

In *Every Man out of his Humour* he returns however to
his former experiment, with results that on the whole are less
successful. It is patchy: Fastidius Brisk is one of the liveliest
of his characters, but the play as a whole is dull, having fallen
heavily into the great trap of the humour-comedy, the use of
an action too obviously designed merely to show the bees in
its people's bonnets. Jonson's great handicap is a certain
chilliness of the imagination: he seldom develops fire enough
to fuse his elaborate detail to a unity, and he is apt not only
to let you hear the creak of the machinery but to take a
positive pleasure in waving the spanner and oilcan in your
face. In fact this play suffers more than any of his from the
restless self-consciousness of its presentation. It is ushered
in by '*Asper* the presenter or author,' and his two friends, in
a long discussion, explaining elaborately what kind of play it

is to be, in a way that reduces it from an intelligent entertainment to a classroom theorem: they reappear between the acts, worrying home each point, and lest anything escape us, each character in the dramatis personæ is introduced, as with Mr. Shaw, by an elaborate (and non-dramatic) description,[1] amusing enough to the reader, but in itself a confession that the play will not suffice unaided to our acquaintance with them. It is a sort of extension of the tiresome trick of using label-names (Deliro, Shift, Fallace, etc.) a habit found before Jonson – indeed it comes from the morality – but by him established as a sort of skin-disease of English literature that lasted right up to the elaborate facetiousness of Thackeray and Trollope, with 'Mr. Nearthewinde' and 'Lady Jane Sheepshanks, daughter of the Marquis of Southdown' – which the *Nineteenth Century*, within this present one, thought very witty, though I believe the actual use was dead by the late nineties. But before Meredith the only great writers of fiction who avoid it completely are the women.

Cynthia's Revels is humour-comedy still, but with a dash of Lyly in its inspiration. It is dull to us for precisely the same reason that made it lively in its own day, the fact that it satirizes not general literary affectations but individual men of letters, slightly disguised in a masquerade of Greek divinities. The satire has point and vigour: it might be amusing if we knew and cared more about the people: and when it hits at a

---

[1] FASTIDIUS BRISK: A neat, spruce, affecting courtier, one that wears his clothes well and in fashion; practises by his glass how to salute; speaks good remnants, notwithstanding the bass viol and tobacco; swears tersely and with variety; cares not what lady's favour he belies, or great man's familiarity: a good property to perfume the boot of a coach. He will borrow another man's horse to praise, and backs him as his own. Or, for a need, can post himself into credit with his merchant, only with the jingle of his spurs and the jerk of his wand.

recurrent type it is amusing still. It shows Jonson's resource-
fulness (like Mr. Shaw's again) in arresting the attention by
some lively device that has nothing to do with the play: it
opens with a group of boy actors tumbling on to the stage,
each clamouring to speak the prologue, and in their chatter
taking off very neatly and tellingly the various types of playgoers, some of whom, to our sorrow, are still with us. But
for the modern auditor there is not much, and for the modern
reader little more, except a trio of Ben's loveliest songs. Its
epilogue, in the key of the famous prologue to *Every Man in
His Humour*, ends with the well-known

'By God, 'tis good, and if you like't, you may,'

which no doubt made the audience sit up as effectually as 'Not
bloody likely.'

The Poetaster is the second campaign of the same war,
though here the mask for the satire is not Olympus, but
Augustus' court. It is closer-knit and more coherent than
the other, with the fine stately verse in it, weighty and forceful rather than melodious, that he was to use in his two
Roman tragedies. Again it suffers from too temporary an
interest. It is a brilliant piece of work, but rather dead now.

There is more life in the additions to *The Spanish Tragedy*.
The play was one that he obviously did not like: yet nothing
of his shows greater imagination than the scene with the
Painter, or the others of Hieronimo's mad grief for his
murdered son.

Of his own tragedies, *Sejanus* and *Catiline*, one comes
before, the other just after, the three great comedies that are
his zenith. Both plays are characteristic, from the choice of
subject onwards, and like his comedies they are written
according to a carefully worked-out theory, that makes them

markedly unlike the tragedy of his contemporaries. The historical play had long, of course, been popular, and naturally it had at times a classical subject: you find that as far back as the reign of Henry VIII, before whom was played an interlude of Troilus and Cressida. But Jonson's are classical in more than subject. He brought to them a scholarly accuracy, not only of atmosphere, as in *Julius Cæsar* and *Coriolanus*, but of detail: and further, he handled them, as nearly as his theatre would permit, in the classic method. As a scholar, in fact, he is on the level of Tennyson or Gray or Milton: but the shadow of antiquity is apt rather to pale his work. The plays are so to speak more closely Roman than Shakespeare's, but they are also considerably less human. It is the easier to make the comparison in that the theme underlying the subject is one that haunted the Elizabethan stage – the evil of an individual ambition launching its country in the ruinous stream of civil war. Not only had they the Wars of the Roses in their mind, as near them as the French Revolution is to us, and like it popular history that an audience would recognize as the modern film audience recognizes an allusion to Madame Guillotine: since then, to drive home the moral, was the turmoil of Tudor succession at home, and in France religious war and persecution, while Scotland was a continued object-lesson. Both plays, however, break with the common form. The Elizabethan chronicle-play as a rule is a loose-jointed affair, generally rather rambling, though the form is capable in the right hands of the magnificent symphonic co-ordination of *Antony and Cleopatra*. Here, for a change, is a considerable hankering after the famous Three Unities: *Sejanus*, indeed, does actually observe the Unity of Place, and the Unity of Action is shown not only in the very careful development of a coherent and co-ordinated sequence of events, but in refusal to mix tragedy with comic relief or even with the battles and pageantry to which the form naturally lent itself – for which, indeed, as in *Henry VIII*, the play might be a mere excuse. In *Catiline* he uses the classic chorus to explain and comment upon the action: in *Sejanus* he is not as orthodox as that, though he apologizes for its absence. They are both fine stately, shapely things, forceful enough and dignified but rather cold. It is probable that given a good company, their stagecraft and the emotional enrichment of the living presences would carry them yet upon the boards: but they have never been much beloved as readers' plays, for all their weight of thought and stately verse.

Between the two Roman plays (in the years, that is, of Shakespeare's great tempestuous tragedies, from *Othello* to a little after *Coriolanus*) come the three comedies that are the high water mark of Jonson's genius. The first of them is *Volpone, or The Fox*. Again the classical infusion shows, for the ultimate source of it, likely enough, is Lucian, and the drawing of the tricked trickster and his scheming servant has certainly much in it that looks like Plautus. The core of the play is the Fox himself, the wealthy miser who sends out false stories that he is mortally ill, so as to make his parasites expose themselves: succeeds, but in his success stumbles on ruin. To this is tacked rather loosely a sort of subplot of the humours of the affected traveller Sir Politic Would-be and his learned lady, who anticipates Molière's *Précieuses*. (Indeed there is a good deal of resemblance to Molière in Jonson almost anywhere, though he lacks the humanity of the great Frenchman.) It is a grim play, for the biting acid of the satire touches not folly or affectation, but actual vices that are bleakly hideous. Indeed, their uniform depth is a dram-

has, *more Jonsoniano*, given away from the beginning: which
is a pity, for the plot, tight, lucid, and compact, is a very
model of its kind. The central action is handled with such
verve that we readily grant the primary postulate, Morose's
horror of noise, though no reason is given for it: and it is
further enriched with a gallery of excellent minor figures –
Sir Amorous Lafoole, the silly scholar Daw, the college
of 'independent' ladies who prove that the New Woman of
the 'nineties (like other startling innovations, such as the
amateur prostitute of the last ten years' comedies) was by no
means so new as either she or her denunciators considered.[1]
The mark of the play's satire is now not vice but affectation,
so that it has more sparkle than *Volpone*, if less of the latter's
grim Hogarthian power. We can laugh at them without
loathing, and on the whole that is a better mood for comedy.

The greatest of the three is *The Alchemist*. In its own day
it perhaps owed some of its popularity to its topical reference
being a skit on the Elizabethan equivalent to the charlatan,
exploiters of psycho-analysis or auto-suggestion. The theme
brings it midway between the others: it is a study not of
silliness or affectation but of frank knavery – yet not the dour
bleak vices of *Volpone*, but a cheery roguery like Peachum's.
Lovewit, a city gentleman, goes out of London, leaving his
house to the care of his knavish servant Face. Face takes
a couple of partners, Subtle the alchemist and Doll Common,
a lady of the same profession as Doll Tearsheet, and nearly
as lively if not so likeable: and the three set up a coney-catching establishment whose dupes give Jonson brilliant chances
for the humour-comedy. The partners are not always amic-

---

[1] There is a perfect specimen of the 'modern flapper' in *Pride and
Prejudice* (1813), complete even to her trial trip for matrimony. And
you can find Mr. Coward's heroine in Maria Edgeworth (*ob.* 1849).

able: the play opens with a really first-class row between the men, with Doll at first attempting to make peace and then screaming them into silence with a volley of red-hot abuse. Amity restored, we see them in the practice of their art, Face and Doll collecting the victims and bringing them to Subtle to be fleeced. The central and greatest of them – perhaps the most memorable of all Jonson's characters – is Sir Epicure Mammon, who hunts for the Philosopher's Stone so that he may have gold to his desire. Jonson has achieved here something far greater than the vivid surface realism of his general work. Sir Epicure has the outreaching desires of the Renaissance that are in Marlowe: and one can see in him how the flame of Faustus has been prostituted, till he becomes a sardonic showing of that gorgeous Renaissance spirit dying in ugliness and dirt for lack of responsibility to any fundamental ethic. In the play he is duped magnificently, like many others, including two solemn Puritans. But then comes vengeance, for Surly sees through the coney-catchers, and brings back the master of the house, who turns them out and – calmly bags the loot.

Bartholomew Fair has even more of Hogarth-come-to-life in it. On a slender thread of farcical citizen-comedy there is strung a roaring piece of broadly comic manners-painting: and the fact that the whole is the adventures of a family party of very strait-laced Puritans gives Jonson a chance for sardonic incongruity that he does not miss. The portrait of the saintly brother Zeal-of-the-Land Busy is matched by the Comstockery of the dirt-hunting magistrate Overdo, whose prowling lands him by the others in the stocks, whence he is released swearing a vengeance that leads to the public discovery of his own most respectable spouse in, to put it mildly, some queer company. It is not a play for anyone of squeamish

F

delicacy: but there is an enormous vigour in it that makes it, to my taste, considerably preferable to the anæmic nastiness of the Restoration.

This verve and pace, and a certain hard brilliant glitter, are the main qualities of Jonson's plays. In spite of his close and outspoken observation, the strength and vigour that embody it, they lack the rich humanity that is the glory not only of Shakespeare but of Dekker or Heywood, men who are intellectually and technically Jonson's inferiors. One never quite escapes from the sense that his people, closely as he has caught external tricks of speech and action, are created less from a birth in the imagination than from a formula in the intelligence. The very cleverness of his tight swift plots but adds to this, and his humour-theory of the drama, though undoubtedly it gives us vivid types, works in with his devotion to the unities to cut him off from the greatest glory of the dramatist, the portrayal of the growth and change of character under the chemistry of changing circumstance. For this reason, too, he lacks the power of handling tragic conflict: his people are always psychologically static. It is perhaps some consciousness of this that makes him prefer, when he can, the Unity of Time. Another point, not in itself and necessarily a defect, but remarkable, is the absence of poetry in his main dramatic work – remarkable not only because poetry was in the very air of the theatre, but because he himself could write it, and with a lovely grace, in masque and lyric. The verse of his tragedies, and when he requires it, of his comedies, moves with fine dignity: but save in the strange marred fire of Sir Epicure Mammon's concupiscence, he lacks the glow and colour of his neighbours – even the sombre rembrandtesque of Chapman. He is essentially a black-and-white man: though his black and white recalls very often Hogarth, or the terrible Raemaker we have forgotten.

His plays held the stage until the nineteenth century, and he had much influence on his successors, not only on the comedy of the Restoration, but on the later satirists, especially Swift: and perhaps too on Fielding and Smollett of the novelists, though Fielding, well as that excellent magistrate knew his London, is always at the heart a countryman. There is a trace of him – or a parallel with him at all events – in the literary member for Cockaigne, Charles Dickens, not only in subject-matter but in method of creating character, though Dickens has more imagination and less intellect. The successor who most resembles him, however, is Mr. Shaw, not only in the preference for lively intellectualized talk over action or the portrayal of emotion, but in such things as, again, the method of creating character – their almost photographic sense of external detail and the phrases of colloquial speech, and their power of using these to give a convincing surface to a personage based not so much on imaginative insight into human experience and human reaction to that experience, as on a formulation of the author's convictions regarding some aspect of human conduct considered generally. Both give a full canvas of boldly-drawn images in rapid and interesting movement: and in both we are left at the end with a sense that the canvas is flat, a diagram in two dimensions, that veils only the dramatist's immediate self. Yet both, within these definite limitations, have the same dry certainty of touch, and the knack of setting their flat figures moving with a brilliant liveliness that seldom fails: and oddly enough, both have the same quaint truculent self-consciousness and inability to take themselves for granted – and the same power of exploiting it to catch an audience.

Like Jonson, GEORGE CHAPMAN was a keen classical scholar, and a dramatist in whose plays the intellectual predominates: it may be added, too, he had Jonson's arrogance. Yet the whole 'feel' of his work is very different: instead of his companion's clear bold outline there is a sort of smoky incandescence that glows at times to a great shadowed splendour. One could hardly say that more than perhaps one of his plays is dramatically speaking good as a whole: but his two chief tragedies have splendid scenes in them, and something of the towering quality he had caught from his immediate master Marlowe. They have a smoulder of imagination that one does not find for more than a stray flash in Jonson: but as with Marlowe again, it is not an imagination specifically dramatic. It is magnificent, but too purely reflective, too philosophically meditative, to express itself naturally and inevitably in terms of action: and he has a difficulty in getting inside any personality but a central one which, as in Marlowe, is pretty much a *persona* for his own: his greatest plays have only one real character apiece in them, to which the others are no more than background, with little sense of individual life.

His dramatic writing comes late in a career that did not itself begin early, setting him with men younger than himself. In point of fact he was five years the senior of either his friend Marlowe or his enemy Shakespeare, a year Greene's elder, and only by that much younger than Peele or Kyd. Yet though he thus belongs by birth to the time of the Wits, his first work published, even non-dramatic, did not appear till two of them were dead. His long life lasted until 1634, eight years before the closing of the theatres, so that although he was nearly thirty when Tamburlaine first strode through Marlowe's verse, he lived into the year of *Comus*. We know that he was an established dramatist in 1598, but only two plays of his that fall within the 'nineties have survived. These are *The Blind Beggar of Alexandria* and *An Humorous Day's Mirth* – poor stuff the pair of them. Essex was his patron, and he probably shared the clouding of his fortunes: but his translation of Homer won him the favour of the brilliant young Prince Henry, and he wrote court masques that Jonson praised, though only one poor specimen has survived. The plays we have, besides those two that I have mentioned, come between 1605 and 1631. He wrote comedy as well as tragedy, but it was not his element: by far his best work there is his share in *Eastward Ho* with Marston and Jonson. Of his independent comedies the best is *All Fools*, in the same year, 1605: and the most one can say of that is 'competent hackwork.' The plot is on the lines of a French farce, with a mildly risqué innuendo as substitute for the almost completely absent humour. Its entanglements move lucidly, and something is generally happening, but it is thin and not particularly lively. *The Gentleman Usher* and *Monsieur d'Olive* come the next year, and are not very dissimilar. The late *May Day* and *The Widow's Tears* are feebler still.

Where his real merit lies is in his tragedies, especially in two curious and interesting pairs of plays in the old Marlowe-Senecan tradition: Mr. Boas indeed suggests, and with much likelihood, that the idea of them may have sprung from an early collaboration of Chapman in *The Massacre at Paris*,[1] mainly ascribed to Marlowe. As there, we have episodes from almost contemporary French history, presented with an almost Jonsonian indifference to popularity, for his Henri de

[1] It was Chapman who finished Marlowe's incompleted narrative poem, *Hero and Leander*.

Valois is a much more respectable person than he appears in
cold historic fact, let alone in contemporary English popular
tradition: and even Guise has his qualities. The plays in
question are *Bussy d'Amboise* in 1607, *The Revenge of Bussy
d'Amboise* five years later, and in between them *The Con-
spiracy of Charles Duke of Biron* and *The Tragedy of Charles
Duke of Biron,* published in 1608 and dealing with incidents
that had actually taken place in 1602. Later he tried his
hand at classical tragedy, in *Cæsar and Pompey,* published in
1631 : and he had a share in others, notably *Chabot Admiral of
France,* published after his death as a collaboration with a
much younger man, Shirley. Two rather gory anonymous
plays, also published after his death, have been attributed to
him, not very certainly: *Alphonsus Emperor of Germany* and
Revenge for Honour, the latter with an Oriental setting. But
it is by the Bussy and Biron plays that he endures as a
dramatist.

Even there his main virtues are not always the specifically
dramatic ones. All his best plays are powerfully conceived,
and seen, one would think, as wholes, not as mere strings
of event: but the conception is sometimes masked in confusing wordiness, and he cannot order the action so as to
present it clearly without a certain creaking of machinery.
Yet when he has achieved a situation, the scene that
clinches it has often enough a superb and gloomy strength,
though less from emotional power than from a deeply
intellectual imagination: the emotion he best understands is
arrogance.

The Bussy plays are much the most dramatic. The first of
them, indeed, should stage effectively, if well produced. It
shows the rise to fortune of an adventurous poor gentleman,
and the disaster of his fall and death. The people of the

action bear real names, of Chapman's own contemporaries,[1] and the action itself follows pretty closely on historic fact, though the real Bussy, a brilliant young soldier, was not apparently as poor as Chapman, for dramatic purposes, makes out. There are some liberties in the presentation of character – rather astonishing liberties for an Englishman born and bred under Elizabeth, since they include the whitewashing of Henri III and at least a certain bleaching of the Duke of Guise, who though concerned in the plot to murder Bussy, is given motive for it in Bussy's public flouting and arrogant public courtship of his Duchess. Bussy himself is something the D'Artagnan, but a philosopher too of the school of Diogenes, his blunt outspokenness backed by a handy rapier. After his rise he makes love, successfully, to Tamyra de Montsurry (Montsoreau) who has repulsed the advances of his patron Anjou: the affair, discovered, brings about his death, for Tamyra is tortured by her husband into writing a letter which serves as bait to bring him to a fatal ambush. The whole is a curious alternation of swift violent action and long meditative speeches: its emotional colour and dramatic method recall a blend of *Tamburlaine* and *The Spanish Tragedy*. It is indeed most frankly Senecan: Bussy's death-speech is full of echoes from that of Seneca's dying Hercules on Œta: but essentially, Bussy and the poetry are Chapman's own.

It would play admirably, I believe, if one could only find actors to speak the verse – Bussy's opening speech on poverty, with its 'Man is a torch blown by the wind,' the Messenger's long description of the sixfold duel with the

---

[1] The real Bussy – Louis de Clermont Bussy d'Amboise – was only ten years Chapman's senior, and Chapman was twenty at the time of the events in the play.

mignons[1] (one wonders if Chapman made it take place 'off stage' for the delight of telling it in verse) or Tamyra's invocation to Night:

> 'Now all ye peaceful regents of the night,
> Silently-gliding exhalations,
> Languishing winds and murmuring falls of waters,
> Sadness of heart, and ominous secureness,
> Enchantments, dead sleeps, all the friends of rest
> That ever wrought upon the life of man,
> Extend your utmost strengths, and this charmed hour
> Fix like the Centre! Make the violent wheels
> Of Time and Fortune stand, and great Existence,
> The Maker's treasury, now not seem to be,
> To all but my approaching friends and me.'

There is the same smoky incandescent poetry in the strange conjuring scene where Tamyra's confessor, who has played go-between, conjures up Behemoth, and again in Bussy's speech, when he is warned of death —

> 'Terror of darkness! O thou King of Flames
> That with thy music-footed horse dost strike
> The clear light out of crystal on dark earth' —

or the whole of his speech as he dies, defiantly standing, propped on his sword.

The Revenge of Bussy d'Amboise is very similar in atmosphere, and even more closely Senecan in method. Its main action portrays the avenging of Bussy by his brother Cler-

---

[1] The duel as it stands is Chapman's invention. But Brantôme tells how Bussy and a certain St.-Phal fell out over the jet embroidery on a muff, and how Bussy and five friends fought St.-Phal and an equal number of the Scots Guard.

mont and his sister Charlotte, who compass Montsurry's death, but are betrayed by Baligny, Charlotte's husband. Clermont achieves his end, despite Baligny, but will not survive the murder of Guise his master: and the play ends with a strange mourning group of women over Clermont's body – his sister who has shared his vengeance, Bussy's old love Tamyra, his victim's widow, and the Countess of Cambrai, his own lover, who has wept herself blind in sorrow for his downfall, and so arrives too late to save his life.[1] The Senecan tradition is followed in Bussy's vengeful ghost, and in the dance of spectres round the dead Montsurry. Clermont himself, more meditative than his brother, has a reminiscence of Hamlet in him. In spite of violent action, there is less dramatic quality than in the *Tragedy*: but there is the same kind of poetry in lines like

 'The black soft-footed hour is now on wing
  Which for my just wreak ghosts shall celebrate:'

and one may mention that its dedicatory epistle throws an interesting light on Chapman's theory of tragedy, which is strongly ethical.

 The double play of *The Duke of Biron* is not as in the D'Amboise pair a play and sequel, but one long play in ten acts, or rather in nine, for the second of *The Tragedy* showed the Queen of France in a rather dubious light, and was censored by demand of the French ambassador. The subject again is the fall of a king's favourite – one even more spectacular than Bussy's. The king is Henri IV this time, and Biron a brilliant soldier-courtier, Marshal of France. He

---

[1] There is less history and more invention here. Clermont d'Amboise is a quite imaginary character, though Bussy's sister Renée did marry a De Baligny, and did desire to avenge her brother on Montsoreau.

grows drunk with his own success, filled with the ὕβϱις of
the Renaissance, the secure and passionate arrogance that to
the Greeks was the main cause of tragedy: so he conspires
against the King, is degraded and slain. Yet as a whole it is
more epic than dramatic: it lacks, even curiously, the action
of the others, although it has again their poetry. Biron's
great speech of passionate exultation when he defies the
astrologer who foretells his end has the spirit of the 'four
elements' speech in *Tamburlaine*: indeed, much of the play
is like Marlowe middle-aged.

> 'Give me a spirit that on this life's rough sea
> Loves t' have his sails filled with a lusty wind
> Even till his sail-yards tremble, his masts crack,
> And his rapt ship run on her side so low
> That she drinks water, and her keel ploughs air.
> There is no danger to a man who knows
> What life and death is: there's not any law
> Exceeds his knowledge: neither is it lawful
> That he should stoop to any other law.
> He goes before them and commands them all
> That to himself is a law rational.'

There is the same quality in Henry's speech on kingship –

> 'O Thou that govern'st the keen swords of kings' –

and all through the closing act of Biron's death:

>   'I know besides
> That life is but a dark and stormy night
> Of senseless dreams, terrors, and broken sleeps;
> A tyranny, devising pains to plague
> And make man long in dying, rack his death;
> And death is nothing; what can you say more?

I bring a long globe, and a little earth:
Am seated like the earth, 'twixt both the heavens,
That if I rise, to heaven I rise; if fall
I likewise fall to heaven. What stronger faith
Hath any of your souls? What say you more? . . .
    Why should I keep my soul in this dark light
Whose black beams lighted me to lose myself?'

So, in the play's last lines:

'And so, farewell for ever. Never more
Shall any hope of a revival see me.
Such is the endless exile of dead men.
Summer succeeds the spring: autumn the summer:
The frosts of winter the fallen leaves of autumn:
All these, and all fruits in them, yearly fade,
And every year return, but cursed man
Shall never more renew his vanished face.
        (Down) on your knees then, statists, ere ye fall,
That you may rise again: knees bent too late
Stick you in earth like statues: see in me
How you are poured down from your clearest heavens;
Fall lower yet, mix with th' unmoved Centre,
That your own shadows may no longer mock ye.
        Strike, strike, O strike! Fly, fly, commanding soul,
And on thy wings, for this thy body's breath
Bear the eternal victory of death.'

    Indeed, there is more than a hint of Marlowe in the
strong swooping decasyllables, not fused into the great harmonies of Shakespeare's later work, where the unit is not the
line but the verse-paragraph. Beside and through the Marlowesque blank verse, the reflective passages shift often to a

ringing gnomic couplet that is a good deal more like a very different man from Marlowe – Dryden.

The plays have passion in them, but it is mainly a passion of the intellect, of apprehension rather than experience. Chapman's emotions are intense enough, but the gamut he commands of them is short, and his perceptions, keen as they are, are not of the most delicate. For all his profound thought, one feels a touch of burly ruffian in him. It is this that makes for his narrowness in the drawing of characters: his people have a fierce intensity, but are seldom very clearly individuated. Yet if he was no psychologist he was a poet, and at times he is a dramatist as well.

JOHN MARSTON, like so many of the rest, is rather shadowy as a personality. We know however that he was a lawyer's son, born at Coventry in the late fifteen-seventies, and that he was a graduate of Oxford. His mother was Italian, and there is a strong trace of the Latin in the peculiar quality of his sardonic humour. His literary career is rather curious. He began with satire, took to drama in the last year of the century, and after eight years as a popular and successful dramatist, took orders, and never wrote another play, although he lived till 1634. His tombstone in the Temple bears for its epitaph, *Oblivioni sacrum*.

It is characteristic that his works begin with a couple of satires, still more that the second of them, *The Scourge of Villany*, is dedicated 'To his most esteemed and beloved self.' He took a lively part in the War of the Theatres, to which his chief contribution is *Histriomastix*, a court play written as reply to *Cynthia's Revels*. He had a hand in some others of the kind, and in *Eastward Ho*, which is better than any comedy of his own sole work. Of his own plays, the most notable are *Antonio and Mellida*, a romantic comedy-drama, in 1600; its sequel, *The Revenge of Antonio*; *The Malcontent*, which is his best play, in 1604; and *The Dutch Courtesan* in 1605. *Parasitaster or The Fawn* reads like an imitation of *The Malcontent*. There is little merit in the crude tragedy of *Sophonisba*, and less in *The Insatiate Countess* of 1613, a horror-play à la Webster, with a 'vamp' heroine who murders her successive lovers.

Marston is rather an odd sort of person. Reading him one feels that he comes a decade or so too late, that his real place is somewhere alongside Kyd. He has the casual construction of the early Wits, and his taste in horrors recalls *The Jew of Malta* rather than Ford: he has not the *haut goût* of the Decadents. The dry hard line of his drawing is rather like Jonson's, and he has something of Jonson's fundamental sanity: beneath the rant and gore one is aware of a definite, though never very fine, sense of moral values – morals, however, rather negative. His favourite hero is the man who bluntly denounces the vices and the follies of his milieu, generally in an odd hurtling vehement prose, which is sometimes decidedly effective, but leaves one at others with a suspicion that his Swiftian attitude is too much merely attitude: one seldom feels Swift's white-hot sincerity. As a matter of fact, a sustained and sincere continuance of that outlook would probably be impossible in any man who had not the seeds of madness in him: and Marston seems to have been sane enough.

Antonio and Mellida has touches of real pathos in it, and now and then catches the imagination: but it suffers seriously from Marston's weakness for peopling his plays with characters that have in them something of the monstrous. Most Elizabethan dramatists attempted at one time or another to draw a figure of a cold, extra-human type: Shakespeare achieved it triumphantly and for all time in Iago, and has for pendant to it an interesting little study of a sort of Brummagem imitation of it – a Borgia manqué – in Don John. Besides the innumerable gentlemen who fancied themselves in the rôle, it was a type that had a real existence, especially in Renaissance Italy, with which Machiavelli's description had caused it to be associated in the popular mind: and it shared the fascination that Italy exerted on the English Renaissance, from Wyatt and Surrey onward to John Milton, to say nothing of appealing to the engaging dislike of the Englishman in all ages for his innate racial respectability.

The Revenge of Antonio has been compared to a blend of *The Murder of Gonzago* with *The First Part of Jeronimo*: certainly it has all the Senecan thrills, of ghosts and dumb-shows and a large helping of gore. There are some odd Shakespearian echoes, especially of the two *Richard* plays. Marston never was a very original or creative thinker. He imitates many men, including himself.

The most serious weakness of both plays, however, is one that is endemic in Elizabethan drama of the second quality – an extreme carelessness of probabilities. I do not mean merely that the dramatists deal with events unlikely to befall the staff of a Victorian university, but that they are given to sudden psychological shifts for which no reason can be assigned but that the plot demands them, and to letting the major crisis be solved or (which is not so bad) produced by flagrantly employed coincidence. These faults, of course, were not peculiar to the Elizabethans: few dramatists who have written for a living, and consequently had to produce work in a hurry, are quite free from an occasional surrender. But the bigger men contrive to make us accept them by their stagecraft. Marston and those on his level do not seem to know there is anything wrong.

One sees this even in his best play, *The Malcontent*, which however is by no means bad even on paper, and would probably be better on the stage. It was formerly thought to owe its merit to a collaboration with Webster, but later critics have concluded that Webster's share is only the lively induction. The echoes of Shakespeare are conspicuous here: the hero has a reminiscence of Hamlet in him, the villain a much stronger resemblance to Richard III.

The play combines in a rather interesting fashion the romantic comedy of the *Much Ado* type with the Jonsonian comedy of humours. The Duke of Genoa has been banished and his wife imprisoned: he returns in disguise to the usurper's court as Malevole, the 'malcontent,' a blunt outspoken castigator of manners and morals, with Diogenes' licence to say what he will, a situation which gives Marston his chance for a sardonic presentation of court corruptions, done sometimes with considerable power. Alongside this, to provide the play with action, run the intrigues of the Machiavelian Mendoza, who by making love to the usurper's duchess Amelia, contrives to make her plot her husband's murder. When he thinks his end has been achieved he publicly denounces her, so that he can consolidate his position by marrying the imprisoned Duchess Maria, whose loyalty to her deposed husband gives relief to the grimy motives of most of the rest. Mendoza's machinations are foiled by Malevole, who ultimately returns in triumph to his wife and his dukedom, pardoning the usurper Pietro, who is rather improbably reconciled to his Amelia. Some of the dramatic devices used in it are rather effective. Marston evidently thought so himself, for he repeats the disguised duke in *Parasitaster*.

Probably the best thing he ever did is his share, whatever it was, in *Eastward Ho*, one of the best comedies the age produced. In type it is nearer Jonson, on the whole, than Shakespeare. It joins a jolly manners-painting, in the vein of the Eastcheap scenes of *Henry IV*, to a touch of slightly moralistic comedy of humours. The descent of it is probably in the long run from Plautus through *Ralph Roister Doister*, but it has become thoroughly English, with a memory of the comic parts in the old Mysteries. There are not very many successful plays of its kind, and it is among the greatest of them, ranking with Dekker's *Shoemakers' Holiday*.

It begins with the city humours of the household of the worthy goldsmith Touchstone, who has two apprentices, the estimable (and rather priggish) Golding, who is a good boy, marries his master's daughter, and becomes a dignified Justice of the Peace, all as he ought, and the idle Quicksilver, who takes to riotous living and is sacked, and attempting thereafter to live by his wits as a coney-catching man about town, lands in the Counter and makes (rather *ad hoc*) a pious reformation. Beside them are Touchstone's two daughters, the honest sensible Mildred who marries Golding, and the flighty Gertrude, who wants to be a fine lady, and abetted by her silly mother, greatly enriches the fun by her marriage to Sir Petronel Flash, a needy fortune-hunter who wants her money to fit him out for a venture to the Virginias. Having got her to sign it away, he departs on board ship with some one else's wife: but as he is too drunk to gauge his tide, the wherry capsizes in the river, and her crew and passengers are all ingloriously washed ashore at appropriate points of landing, where in due time they receive their just deserts. The whole has a tremendous swing, and something of the broad Hogarthian humour of *The Alchemist*. But its cheery geni-

ality is not very like Jonson's work in general – in fact it is
oddly unlike the individual work of any of its collaborators,
for its ease and directness of movement have none of Marston's fumbling vehemence, and there is nothing of Chapman's truculent dignity nor of the thin-blooded mechanisms
of his weary comedies. There is an attractive touch, too,
of the spacious days in the captain of Sir Petronel's ship *The
Seagull*, with his tall stories of the golden wonders of America.
Altogether, it is a play clamant for revival. It is too essentially
cheery for the real highbrows, and perhaps too sanitary in its
outlook. But if Mr. Playfair could be induced to try his hand
at the Elizabethans, he would find here something better
worth his while than *The Way of the World*, and – odd as it
sounds – lending itself admirably to some of his most characteristic methods. And the estimable Golding is not at all
unlike dear Lionel!

CHAPTER SIX

SHAKESPEARE'S COMPANIONS. II

DEKKER. HEYWOOD

'A fair lively painted picture of the life.'
ROGER ASCHAM, *The Schoolmaster.*

✳

THE cheery kindliness of *Eastward Ho* is one of the most
conspicuous qualities in the engaging work of THOMAS DEK-
KER. As far as the facts of his life go he is one of the least-
known of the whole brotherhood: but his personality shows
lovably through his plays. As a dramatist he has some splendid virtues, balanced by most egregious defects. With only a
fraction of Shakespeare's range or power, and with nearly none
of his miraculous artistry, there is in him the same generous
sanity, the free and sunlit air, that are the atmosphere of
Shakespeare's comedies. The two men he resembles most in
outlook are Chaucer and Fielding, the former especially in his
kindliness, his sense of pathos and of a frank and jolly humour,
touched often with an exquisite grace of poetry: the songs in
his plays can stand with those of Shakespeare or Fletcher,
which is as much as to place them with the loveliest of their
kind. But he suffers badly from too great an output: he gives
one the impression nearly always of having written in a tearing
hurry, with the printer's devil ready at his elbow, and perhaps
a dun or two upon the stairs.

We know neither where nor when he was born, nor when
he died. He was probably rather younger than Shakespeare,
and may have been of Dutch extraction. Whatever he was by
descent, by adoption he was certainly a Londoner – a Lon-

doner as Lamb or Dickens were. He had cause enough to
know the underside of London: one gathers that he was a
shiftless, kindly soul, more ready to give his last shilling to a
beggar than to offer it on account for the grocer's bill. One
would call him an Elizabethan Goldsmith, only he is not
sentimental: it was not a quality of his immediate generation,
and he has no more of it than his companions, though he
championed 'all that were desolate and oppressed.' He might
have been a very great dramatist if he had ever taken time to
be an artist, for along with his immense vitality, his frank,
clear-headed and warm-hearted observation, go a most graceful and gracious fancy, an ear for the cadence both of colloquial
speech and of lyric poetry, a sense of humour, and an eye for a
dramatic situation. Great gifts: but he was always in a hurry.

He tried his hand at all manner of things, from a jest-book
to a volume of fine prayers. A lot of his work – and probably
more that is lost – is in the pamphlets that were Elizabethan
journalism: and the descriptions of the less reputable sides of
life in *The Gull's Hornbook* prepare the way for the more respectable *Tatler* of the eighteenth century. The satire of it is
in Chaucer's key, shrewd, open-eyed, but not at all unkindly,
as far from hatred as from all illusion. His plays are fairly
numerous, though in the fashion of the time he wrote a good
many of them in collaboration. He shared with Middleton in
The Roaring Girl (a jolly thing), with Massinger in *The Virgin
Martyr*, and probably with Ford in *The Sun's Darling*, which
is less a play than a kind of moral masque. An anonymous
play of 1603 called *Patient Grissil* has pretty certainly got his
hand in it – Grissil herself and the songs are unmistakable:
and another, *The Witch of Edmonton*, is probably by Dekker
and Ford, with help from a third man who may be Rowley.
Of the plays that are all his, the best-known, and the best, in

ascending order, are *Old Fortunatus*, a fantastic fairy-tale con-
coction, chaotic to a degree, but with real charm in it, *The
Shoemakers' Holiday*, in 1599, and a double play, *The Honest
Whore*, published five years later.

The *Shoemakers' Holiday* is about the greatest thing of its
own kind, except perhaps *Eastward Ho*. It is a jolly kindly
bustling affair with an enormous verve to it, filled with a
humour never very subtle but always singularly fresh and
clean: there is a certain breadth about it often, but none of that
weary tossing of dirt for dirt's sake that so many of the group,
still more their juniors, are so unsophisticated as to take for
mirth. Indeed it has the spirit of the Canterbury Prologue,
though its expression is more robustious than Chaucer's: the
bluff master-shoemaker Sim Eyre goes through it like a
breeze, and is one of the great figures of Elizabethan comedy,
with a headlong gaily-coloured speech that sets him in the
company of Falstaff. Unless one is a horridly superior person
it is impossible not to share in his own delight in himself, and
we are as pleased as he when he is elected Sheriff and comes
home to show off his gown to his wife and bring her a new
French hood to celebrate.

About him are his wife, who is Mrs. Quickly in happier
circumstances, and the lively journeymen who adore him and
continually pretend they are going on strike, but never do. To
set the action moving there is a slight love-story of the courtier
Lacy who woos the Mayor's daughter in the disguise of a
Dutch shoemaker: and to point the humour, a touch of pathos
in the history of Ralph and his wife Jane — the young newly-
married journeyman called up to the wars, leaving reluctantly
but in no cowardly spirit, among the farewell gifts of his
kindly shopmates, and returning to find his wife has dis-
appeared. She is found again, supporting herself with honest

loyalty, having been nearly heartbroken by a false rumour of Ralph's death. Lacy and his Rose, Ralph and his Jane, do not provide a very elaborate story, but their affairs make the frame for a very lively crowded action, that ends as it should with Sim Eyre feasting the prentices of London on his accession to the dignity of Mayor. It has some delectable songs in it too —

'Oh the month of May, the merry month of May'

and the splendid shout of

> 'Cold's the wind and wet's the rain,
> St. Hugh be our good speed.
> Ill is the weather that bringeth no gain
> Nor helps good hearts in need.'

The Shoemakers' Holiday is a fine play in one particular kind: *The Honest Whore*[1] is nearly as fine a one in another, although it has Dekker's faults as well as his virtues. It is a double play, in two five-act parts, each with plot and sub-plot: and it would have gained enormously if he had divided his material otherwise and made two separate disconnected plays, one of citizen-humour-comedy from the sub-plots, which would have been a very poor thing, and one serious play from the main plots, which would have been far from that. It would be very easily possible, and considerably more than pardonable, for a modern manager to make the division: indeed it surprises me that nobody has done so, for there are some splendid acting scenes in it, and telescoped thus it would yield a shapely and coherent action, manageable in length.

As it stands, of course, it is a glaring example of a common and very tiresome trick of the Elizabethan drama, and one

---

[1] *Honest* in Elizabethan English, when applied to a woman, means chaste, 'respectable.'

which was a major cause of the violent reaction against it
when French influence came in: namely, that of putting
alongside the main plot of a serious play a sub-plot of low
comedy barely connected with it, and often most perfunctorily
written. The fault of course is not solely due to artistic per-
versity or even ignorance: it springs from economic pressure.
The close connection of the dramatist with the theatre was
excellent in many ways, but it had its dangers, one of the
worst being the fact that the author was generally writing for
a particular stock company, and had to find adequate parts for
its important members, of whom a principal was the low
comedian. As a rule they threw the sop in anyhow, with an
extremely manifest bad grace: one man alone accepted the apparently ruinous condition, kept to it, and made it an integral
and glorious part not only of chronicle or romantic comedy
– who wants to leave out Falstaff or Dogberry or Sir Toby? –
but even of his greatest tragedies: the Gravedigger, the Porter,
and the Fool, are among the finest dramatic devices in *Hamlet*, *Macbeth*, and *Lear*. But I cannot think of another example where this unity appears to be even aimed at, and I can
remember only too many that on one scale or another repeat
the frank perfunctoriness of *The Honest Whore*. Middleton's
Changeling, for instance, takes its name from a comic plot that
is extremely and rather grimily tedious, hung on with pins to a
tremendous clash of personalities in a profoundly tragic situation.

In Dekker's case we are wise to ignore altogether the sub-
plot of the citizen Candido, who is a sort of Patient Griselda
in breeches, and far more trying than that devastating lady.
The padding is the more flagrant in that the pattern of the
main plot runs through both 'parts.' It is left incomplete and
unsatisfying in the first one, and in the second receives an ironic

twist that adds considerably to its dramatic power. In Part I, Hippolito, who loves the fair Princess Infelice, is deceived by a rather motiveless false story of her death: the play opens effectively with the procession of her feigned funeral. While he is still heart-broken he meets the courtesan Bellafront, a girl of gentle breeding, who has fallen, one gathers, not so much from any real evil in her as from infatuation and levity in the beginning, and then from hopelessness after her first false step. She tries her professional wiles on him, at first in the way of business, and then because she is really attracted by the man. Hippolito, indifferent at first, grows angry and loses his temper, and as he denounces her she sees through his eyes the full ugliness of what she is, and tries to kill herself. Hippolito, startled, checks her, and she resolves that for his sake she will live, and cleanly henceforth, and then, poor soul, makes desperate attempts to win him, foiled by his loyalty to the dead Infelice. She determines then that at least she will do as he would have her, and 'makes an honest woman of herself' by marrying her original seducer, the worthless Matheo: the motive of selection, not because she has any lingering regard for him, but because he was the first, is not ill taken. Matheo refuses, but is won to it by an improbable trick, much below the rest of the serious action, and Hippolito is restored to his recovered Infelice, with her father's consent at last that they should marry. The sequel is a better play as a whole, though with no one scene in it as good as the Bellafront-Hippolito ones in Acts II and III of the First Part. It shows us Bellafront as the wife of Matheo, who is a scoundrelly spendthrift and *chevalier d'industrie*. She takes his ill-usage with a loyal patience that is made human, not Griselda-ish, forgiving when he pawns her very gown, and only turning on him when he would send her back to her old profession to make money for him. The situation is complicated by the fact that Hippolito has wearied of his wife and turned to Bellafront, offering her now what she had vainly tried to win. But she loves him well enough to guard his loyalty and her own, in a reversal of their former situation that has a real dramatic poignancy.

The great character all through is Bellafront. Dekker has drawn her very livingly and with a fine sane comprehension: we feel her charm and fundamental goodness, but she is not sentimentalized in any way. The background of Part II, Act II is like the *Harlot's Progress* made into drama. Yet what he achieves with it is reality, not 'realism': he is as free from the sentimentally sordid as from the sentimentally sugary. Except for one small episode at the end of Part I, which unfortunately is flagrant 'stage,' her character is true to life throughout – truer indeed than the action that surrounds it, for the machinations of Infelice's father are quite incredible, though they give rise to some good acting scenes. Of the other characters, Bellafront's father Friscobaldo has been praised, though I do not find myself enthusiastic over him. Matheo has life, and there is a certain graciousness in Infelice – Dekker had a considerable knack of drawing charming women. Hippolito, in print at least, is a little stiff, but the rôle of Joseph, particularly of reproachful Joseph, is difficult to carry off with dignity, and one does not like him the better for his volte-face: the objection, however, is really to the person and not the 'character,' and he would give an actor opportunities.

For all his obviously first-hand knowledge of the underworld, there is a kind of sweet-natured quality in Dekker that is most attractive. He has a compassionate kindliness always, especially to those whom the world contemns: but his deep comprehension of their side of things is never allowed to muddle his moral values. No man – or woman – was wholly evil to Thomas Dekker: but evil was, and he has none of that hankering after its cheap picturesqueness that we find a few years later in the decadents.

A temperament that is not very dissimilar shows through the work of his part-namesake THOMAS HEYWOOD.[1] He also has the same sense of the dramatic values of an emotional situation, and the same sunny geniality that yet can look on the darker side of life and neither shirk it nor be subjugated. And unhappily he has Dekker's faults, too, of hurried careless-ness and slovenly construction: he had an enormous facility and owns to having had a hand in two hundred and twenty plays. I wish that more of them had chanced to survive: we have no guarantee that his best ones did, and I would wade cheerfully through a good many duds to find one as good as *A Woman Killed with Kindness*.

We know a little more about him than we do about Dek-ker, but not much. He was probably of a rather higher social class: the type of character in which he excels is that of the country gentleman, neither rich nor poor and neither lout nor courtier, who was the very backbone of the nation, and who led and officered those glorious desperate ventures that make the commercial history of the time read like the *Morte d'Arthur* – on which book, by the way, a lot of the venturers would have been bred. (I wonder if we shall do as well on *Tarzan?*) He was born in Lincolnshire in 1572, and took his degree at Cambridge. We know that he went on the stage – Henslowe mentions him in 1596 – and he seems to have loved

---

[1] Not to be confused with the early John Heywood who wrote inter-ludes.

his profession: at all events his connection with the theatre lasted some forty years. He entered the King's service in 1634, but we do not know when he died. Though not a Londoner by birth he was one by adoption, and seems to have loved the city.

Like Dekker he was essentially a dramatist of the popular theatre, and it is perhaps to this that his plays owe what most spoils them. If his enormous energy and the touch of real dramatic genius in him had been balanced by any deliberate artistic conscience, he would have been great instead of merely notable. He spoils himself with a huddled fluency. Both he and Dekker had creativeness enough for half a dozen dramatists, and – with exceptions that are sadly few in number – neither has the constructiveness that should go with it, and this although Heywood has an excellent eye for a situation, and nearly always opens a play admirably.

His non-dramatic work is small, and not important. A full list of his huge *théâtre* is impossible, and most of it, in any case, is lost. There is no collected edition, and the extant texts are an unholy mess: like many other men of his day he had no conscience about proof-reading or perhaps (and likely enough) no chance of it. We know at all events that he produced a steady stream of every kind of play then known to the stage – chronicle-history, romantic drama, pageants, mythological plays, and comedies of manners, with assorted combinations of these modes. He was not inclined to tragedy, however: there is a vein of real pathos in him, and he can handle deep strong feeling with nobility, but he is seldom passionate in the more fiery ways: his emotion glows, but never breaks to flame. He has a kind of natural daylight quality.

He draws the life of the city well enough, but his special strength, as I have said, is in the English country gentleman:

his men *are* gentlemen, by instinct and breeding, and not by any fine-drawn stage convention. He gives the type not only in its normal milieu but in what after all was the scarcely less normal one of glorious venturing by sea and land. Captain Spencer's Odyssey in *The Fair Maid of the West* has something of the quality of Hakluyt.

The least important group of his works, perhaps, is the classical one, which includes a group of four on the Gold, Silver, Bronze, and Iron Ages, dramatizing legends from Homer and Ovid in a fashion that is sometimes both pleasant and racy, though not very dramatic: *Love's Mistress*, a long allegory, more masque than play, of Cupid and Psyche: and *The Rape of Lucrece*, which is really a chronicle-play whose principal theme is the expulsion of the Tarquins, with a Roman gentleman who sings many songs, generally comic (and sometimes ribald, in a fashion rare in Heywood) including one in Dutch and one in Scots, and a most charming aubade with the note of the *little* birds in it.

It links to the English chronicles, such as the double play of *Edward IV*, an involved affair, whose Second Part has no fewer than five separate stories in it, with touches, however, of Heywood's special quality in his handling of Shore, husband of King Edward's mistress, who is like a preliminary sketch for the Master Frankford of his greatest play. Another double play, *If You Know not Me, You Know Nobody*, deals in its first part with Queen Elizabeth's early dangers, in its second with the Armada. It is clumsy and huddled, but with a sincere patriotism.

A Royal King and Loyal Subject and *A Challenge for Beauty* are in the key of romance. The first is a set of variations on the Patient Griselda idea, not very interestingly handled: the second tells of a proud Queen of Portugal who has to admit her beauty vanquished by an English lady, with as sub-plot a contest in generosity between two enemies, that has something of the feel of the *Knight's Tale* in it, of Palamon and Arcyte arming each other before they fight to the death. It is full enough of far-fetched situations, yet remarkably free from the hectic tone that one finds in the handling of such subjects by the school of Beaumont and Fletcher.

The Four Prentices of London, with the Conquest of Jerusalem is a gorgeous mixture of chronicle-history and popular adventure-drama. Guy, Eustace, Tancred, and Gismond, four sons of the crusading Duke of Bouillon, become London prentices, and as such set off to the Crusades and win their spurs, and Guy is finally crowned in Jerusalem. The Jerusalem scenes have a real reverence, but the whole is frankly meant for 'the limbs of Limehouse and the tribulation of Tower-Hill,' and rather asks for Beaumont and Fletcher's delicious parody in *The Knight of the Burning Pestle*.

The romance of it shows again, less fantastically, in *Fortune by Land and Sea, The Fair Maid of the Exchange*, and a double play, *The Fair Maid of the West*, all of which are a blend of romantic adventure with the English domestic drama that shows Heywood at his strongest. *The Fair Maid of the Exchange* is much the worst, being sickly in sentiment – a fault rare with Heywood – and marred also by another only too common with him, in the way in which the heroine's affections are transferred from one man to another simply and obviously because the plot requires it. But some of the scenes have merit, and the cripple hero is rather interesting. *Fortune by Land and Sea* and *The Fair Maid of the West* have a stronger infusion of the adventure element, though the former opens with some excellent English tavern scenes as background to the series of quarrels that sets the action going. *The*

Fair Maid of the West is a sort of dramatized adventure-novel, and a rather jolly one. Its central figure, Bess Bridges, is a charming person, and as 'modern' as all these Elizabethan women are when they are anything beyond lay figures. We see her first (in some capital scenes) as serving-maid in a Plymouth tavern, where her mixture of frankness and modesty attracts her gentleman lover, Captain Spencer. He sails adventuring, leaving Bess mistress of a Cornish tavern, and is taken prisoner by the Spaniards. Bess, meanwhile, has had her own adventures: she is a capable and spirited young woman, well able to look after herself, even to discomfiting, disguised as her own brother, a 'roaring blade' who troubles the peace of her inn. A false story of Spencer's death is brought to her by a treacherous comrade: she sells her property, fits out a ship, and sails privateering to avenge him: but the two are deservedly reunited after many adventures with pirates, Spaniards, and the King of Fez. I am not sure that it would stand the modern stage, but it is pleasant reading, with a fine salt-water quality in the adventures, set off by a real pathos now and then, as in the scene where Bess is forced to part with her 'dead' lover's portrait and then thinks she is going to get it back.

The English Traveller, in spite of its title, is domestic drama, and though not formally a tragedy, is sufficiently grim, showing a trust cruelly betrayed. The hero Geraldine comes home from abroad to find his old love has been married, to a very kindly and generous old man who is good to both of them: and then he learns that she loves him still. They confront their love frankly and honourably: they will not betray her husband who has trusted them, but she promises to marry Geraldine if she is ever free. And then he learns that she has played both him and her husband false, with his own dearest friend. Mrs. Wincott is rather too invertebrate to rouse our emotions very much, but Geraldine has the sense of normal humanity about him that one so often has in Heywood, so rarely in the most of his successors. He makes the situation real and pitiful: but the play is hampered as usual by a stupid sub-plot.

There is English domestic life again, though with far less dramatic quality, in *The Lancashire Witches*, a sort of farcical transcript of a contemporary law-case, and in *The Wise Woman of Hogsden*, the tale of a fortune-telling impostor. But Heywood's greatest essay in domestic drama is *A Woman Killed with Kindness*, which has the same theme as *The English Traveller*, of a trust in a woman's honesty betrayed. A young and deeply loved and trusted wife is false to her husband with his close friend Wendoll, to whom he has shown infinite kindness. It is not Mrs. Frankford's fall that is the main theme, however, but rather Frankford's reaction to it, his pain and shame and anger at betrayal, and the generosity that masters them, till his wife realizes what she has done, and dies of heartbreak. It does not sound a promising theme: it would in fact have been easy to make it 'sobstuff' or to give Frankford a touch of complaisance that would ruin sympathy. Heywood avoids both traps. There is a sense of infinite pity whose gentleness has nothing weak in it: and though the second act, of Mrs. Frankford's downfall, is too hurried to be genuinely effective, the play makes up for it in the intense dramatic quality of Frankford's slow realization and discovery, his gaining of irrefutable proof, his wild outbreak of agony and anger, and then his actual dealing with the culprits. The sub-plot of the feud between Acton and Mountford begins well, but ends with a scene of violent psychological improbability, and as usual, is very loosely attached – or not attached at all – to the main plot: yet even here there is a life about the people that serves to increase the shock we feel at Mountford's calm offer of his sister's honour to pay the debt he owes his sometime enemy. Frankford is excellent all through, but Wendoll and Mrs. Frankford are much less satisfying. Wendoll, indeed, never really comes to life, and though one feels Mrs. Frankford as rather more of a person, her fall is never adequately motivated: she is not, apparently, a light woman by nature, but there is no attempt to show her infatuated like that Elizabethan Edith Thompson, Alice Arden, or even swept off her feet by a gust of passion: she is merely limp. Even so, however, her part has some good touches in it: her 'O Master Wendoll!' shows Heywood's success in conveying the emotional values under the semi-articulate speech of everyday. There is the same thing again in Frankford's heartbroken cry of 'O Nan, Nan!' when he learns her guilt.

Heywood stands apart from most of his equals and contemporaries in that he never attempts, successfully or not, to give reality to great imaginative creations: he chooses rather to give the poignancy of an emotional crisis between quite ordinary normal people. And as a corollary, for all his love of adventure, he is free from any craving for far-fetched violence. It is scenes and not poetry or characters that we remember in his plays. But we remember them.

CHAPTER SEVEN

SHAKESPEARE'S JUNIORS. I

THE TRANSITION. MIDDLETON. ROWLEY. WEBSTER. TOURNEUR

'Touched sublimity at points.'

THOMAS HARDY, *The Woodlanders.*

✱

BETWEEN the men I have described in the last chapter and those who come in this and the next one there is a gap, though of spirit rather than chronology. Indeed Middleton, who with Webster bridges it, is in actual fact a couple of years Heywood's senior, and Marston, whom I have placed with his elders Jonson and Chapman, has already some qualities of their successors.

Yet on the whole, as we pass from Jonson and Chapman, Marston and Heywood and Dekker, to the group that includes Beaumont and Fletcher, Ford and Massinger, we are conscious of a steady change in atmosphere. There are fine plays yet, but there is an autumn in their splendour, and the minors have decay of autumn rather than its colour. Even the greater ones show a good deal of that 'inspiration of the unnatural' which Dr. Saintsbury has well described as 'the Dutch courage of literature,' and which is a common mark of a certain spiritual dullness in both an artist and his audience, as a taste for highly-seasoned food shows a palate that cannot respond to finer stimuli.

In the actual subject-matter of the drama there is a growing tendency to avoid themes which have any connection with real life, and a corresponding search for others whose interest is in far-fetched or surprising situation: and since these situations are what count, the play jolts onward from one to another without much heed to methods of transition. With this goes a more than Senecan joy in violent machinery – mad-houses, elaborate poisonings, and complicated ways of suicide or murder. So also mere lawless love is not high-spiced enough: it must be seasoned further with some ghastly complex treachery or a perversion of the laws of nature.

It is true, of course – indeed, I have remarked already – that just as emotions which seem improbable to many scholars may be real – a point which would save some bewildered comment upon *Hamlet* – so events which seemed impossible in Victorian London (which none the less produced Constance Kent) or Victorian Glasgow (the home of Madeleine Smith, that charming poisoner) were matters of not uncommon fact in Jacobean London or Edinburgh or Paris. There is not much in the maddest of Tourneur to match the whole lurid business of Lady Essex' second marriage, the murder of the Duke of Guise, the death, however gained, of the Master of Ruthven; and the episode of Darnley, Bothwell, and Queen Mary would equal any plot of Webster's, with Moray and Lethington in the best Machiavelian tradition. What is wrong is not that the plays show violent action, but that the obvious reason for showing it is a mere craving not for adventures of the human spirit, but for violence in itself and for its own sake – for violence, too, shown with no implication of any standard of normality.

The natural result is that the dramatists seldom look further than a surface fury, and in consequence, characterization weakens. When the attention of author and audience was devoted to the intricacies of some new and unheard-of method of poisoning, they had not much to spare for the psychology

H

of the victim or his murderer: it was enough to people the play with types that would be recognizable. Indeed, we have at times what is almost a reversion to the personified qualities of the morality. The people are machinery to produce an arresting situation, and as a natural corollary one finds with this no care to keep the characters self-consistent. Since they have their being purely for the sake of the action, they are left very much at its disposal.

The result of this unreality is a fatal lack of sympathy on the dramatist's part for the people whom he should be creating, which results in a similar lack on the part of the audience, who fail to be emotionally stirred. Of course it is true that simple and undeveloped minds regard the hero or heroine as mere masks for themselves as they would like to be, and so prefer those who have no definite or personal identity: the little shop-girl likes to imagine herself playing lead in one of Mr. Arlen's novels, the mild city clerk enjoys himself as the strong silent hero or the pioneer in 'the big open spaces,' though he would squeal with terror if you left him an hour alone on the Moor of Rannoch. But a more developed mind has less of this variety of egoism, and demands, in play or novel, people who have existence in themselves. Yet mere intellectual interest in strange types is equally inadequate: if a play is to be art and not science it must reach our emotions somehow, present to us people and actions in such a way that we have a comprehend-ing sympathy with themselves or at all events with the author's experience of them. We understand them, as we would not understand them in real life, and understanding, we share their feelings for the moment, not merely look on them with pity or disgust. This is not necessarily true of every character, of course. Pandarus, for instance, is meant to rouse an almost physical nausea: and he does. But even in that horrible play, there are people whom one must like as well as pity: it would be a good deal less horrible if one did not. But in, say, *Women beware Women*, which is a very competent play on a subject not very dissimilar, Leantio and Bianca are so contemptibly shallow that one cannot feel it matters what becomes of them: the most powerful emotions stirred in us are disgust or a quite cold scientific curiosity.

The absence of any real emotional quality in these violent plays links with – is partly produced by – another emptiness. Just as it is impossible to make us share a human being's experience of action unless we are made in some measure to share imaginatively his emotion over it, so it is impossible to portray conduct itself in the round, as it were, without some underlying scale of values. And this also is missing. It is not that the plays show evil, merely. It would be difficult, on that point, to outclass Pandarus or Iago. What has happened is that there is no longer any standard. It is not a case of 'evil, be thou my good.' That is as old as *Faustus*, and to say it implies a pretty clear perception not perhaps of good and evil themselves, but of their opposition, and of the will in man to choose between them. What we have in such things as *A Chaste Maid in Cheapside* or the dreary intrigues of Restoration, or some modern, comedy is something different and less sophisticated – something that is more like an ignorance of all three. They give us 'the natural man' with no personal will to guide his animal instincts: and a sufficiently nasty spectacle he always has been. Of course the type exists, and is therefore a legitimate subject for art: but the artist himself needs an intelligence that has been more developed. There is nothing decadent in showing evil triumphant; materially, as in *Tess of the Durbervilles* or *Othello*, spiritually, as in *Macbeth*. Evil does often win, and it is therefore right that art should show its victories.

The decadence comes in when the artist regards the triumph cheerfully, as something natural and insignificant.

The inevitable result of all these things is a difference in the quality of the poetry. One seldom thinks of it now as 'sublime' or 'glorious' or 'magnificent.' The virility has gone, and the poetry is only decorative. It is that, most exquisitely, sometimes. But the beauty is not so much extracted by the imagination as applied by the fancy, 'and the guards' of their wit but slightly basted on.' With this, as one would expect, comes a change in form. The old strong pulses of the rhythm have altered. They strove for freedom, and when it was won they were not big enough to use it. The original 'end-stopped' verse of the Wits, with its tight unyielding hold on the structure of the decasyllable, had suppled to one more flexible, more 'enjambed,' that gave the rhythm of spoken words more naturally. Then this was overdone, and produced a sort of bastard semi-prose, with as reaction, an attempt to pull the sprawling line together with a return to the rhyme the elders had discarded.

As one gathers from all these, the age was wearying, with a spiritual fatigue that issues in a mental one. It shows itself in varying degrees, until there is a sort of sickness of the whole form of Elizabethan drama, and the highbrows of 1660 could only like even Shakespeare with apologies. The candle goes out, and a great age is over. What the Puritans killed was already dead and rotten.

Before the decadence has set in finally, however, there are two men whose minor work shows it plainly enough, but whose greatest ranks with that of any man I have mentioned yet except Shakespeare. The senior and the lesser of the two

1 Galoon.

is THOMAS MIDDLETON, whose work at its best has a lively fancy in comedy and in tragedy a stark power that is not too far behind Webster, and from the purely dramatic, as distinct from the poetic, point of view is ahead of Chapman. He has not the latter's deep meditative poetry, or Webster's strange meteor-flashes in huge darkness: but *The Changeling* at least gives in a manner very sure and economical that ghastly imprisonment in a hopeless self-created situation that is the very core of essential tragedy. I doubt if there are a dozen characters in the whole of Elizabethan drama outside Shakespeare that stand level with Beatrice-Joanna or De Flores in power of both conception and conveyance.

We know little more of him than of the rest. He was born in London about 1570, and died there in 1627. He seems to have been of gentle birth, and may have been a university man, though this is not certain. He was frequently employed in writing the libretti of pageants, and was made City Chronologer in 1620, though the good luck was followed by bad, for in 1624 a political skit on Spain got him imprisoned. Like most of the rest he wrote voluminously: a score or so of his plays survive, and he may have had a hand in more. Many of them were written in collaboration, probably with Rowley, certainly once with Dekker. Their dates and order are as usual very uncertain, but the first we know of is in 1602.

His work falls in three groups, more or less in ascending order of merit, through comedy of manners, romantic comedy, and tragedy. The first set include *Blurt Master Constable*, *A Trick to Catch the Old One*, *A Mad World, my Masters*, *A Chaste Maid in Cheapside*, *More Dissemblers besides Women*, and *The Widow*. They are rattling pictures of city life, with intricate plots, a certain bustling liveliness of incident, and a dialogue that moves easily and quickly. They are the part of Middleton's work where the thinness of the decadence shows most clearly: it is not that they contain scenes of vice or brutality – they do, but so does Jonson – but rather in the implied point of view. At times, however, there is a certain irony that helps him to keep his balance, and he has an eye for cant, fads, cranks, and jargon, that is as joyful as Dekker's, though his tragic side reminds one of Emily Brontë.

These plays are much on a level, and not a high one. Considerably better than any of them is *The Roaring Girl*,[1] in which he was evidently collaborating with Dekker. It is a jolly, racy thing, and Moll Cutpurse its heroine, who was pretty certainly Dekker's creation, is a lively and likeable tomboy who swaggers through its action playing providence to distressed lovers or helping a needy gallant to dodge his creditors. She is a decent lass who can look after herself, and moves unsoiled in very queer company. One regrets that the historic Moll was quite unlike her.

There is a mixture of tragedy and comedy in *The Spanish Gipsy*, a rather lively thing with an echo of *As You Like It*, and in *The Witch*, which has a certain quality of wild fancy, and has further won an adventitious fame as the source of the Hecate interpolations with which some enterprising manager saw fit to embellish *Macbeth*. The tragic element predominates in *A Fair Quarrel*, an interesting play whose main scenes present the curious moral problem of whether an honourable man can fight when he realizes his cause is false, but is sacredly bound not to admit the fact. Putting aside one or two improbabilities, the action is really well handled, with an excellent sense of the stage; the point, of the ethics of the duel, has been grasped by Middleton's imagination; and its hero,

[1] A 'roaring boy' was what the next century called a mohock.

Captain Ager, is a personage. For comic relief, there is the lively picture, in the key of Smollett rather than Hogarth, of the Roaring Boys, where the dialogue bristles with fashionable slang, and we learn what kinds of abuse were the most modish.

Middleton's greatest work, however, comes in his tragedies, though the merit of the best-known three is rather varied. *The Mayor of Queenborough*, which takes its name from a poor sub-plot that seems to be Rowley's, has for its serious side a chaotic but sometimes powerful handling of Vortigern's passion for the fair Rowena, that makes him dishonour and condemn his virtuous wife Castiza. It is an oddly old-fashioned sort of business, even to anticipatory dumbshows that suggest an older generation.

Women beware Women has an ugly plot and still more hideous underplot: but they are handled – except for a rather sticky opening – with a direct and vigorous competence, in both general structure and individual scenes. The people are tolerably convincing, if quite uniformly unpleasant. The horrible Livia and her victim Bianca, the latter's shallow resistance and surrender, her subsequent brazening out of her own shame and determination to extract all the material price of it are done most competently, though it would have given more emotional value to the situation if Bianca's young husband had been man enough to feel her fall, or at least his own wrongs, instead of subsiding cheerfully into a comfortable berth as Livia's kept gallant. The play lacks depth, for one cannot feel these sort of people matter, except for damage they can do their betters: and here there are none. But all the major scenes, especially that of the chess-playing between Livia and the Widow, have a good eye for the dramatic presentment of a situation, and a vivid actuality. The play ends with a lurid wholesale slaughter in a mode that recalls the conclusion of *The Spanish Tragedy*.

By far the greatest work of Middleton is *The Changeling* – again the name comes from a sub-plot which is supposed to be mainly Rowley's, and is uncommonly poor stuff, going far to spoil a play whose serious part is really memorable. It is so slightly tagged on that it could be completely excised without the audience missing it: and in representation, which the serious plot thoroughly deserves, *ought* to be cut.

The main action moves with a straightforward clean-edged power, and the two chief characters are drawn superbly. Beatrice-Joanna loves and is loved by Alsemero: but she is already betrothed to Piracquo, and her father refuses to break off the match. In her headlong passion she catches the first instrument to her hand, her father's needy hanger-on, De Flores, has him murder Piracquo, and is faced then with his demand of herself as price of the service and his silence. She has to submit, and then must purchase his aid in the subsequent deception of the husband she loves, by a continuance of her favours, until chance betrays them both to Alsemero. It sounds, thus summarized, mere horror-mongering: but though it is true that some parts of Act IV are rather grotesque, at any rate to a modern eye, it is given a terrible actuality throughout by the superb drawing of the two chief figures. De Flores is a type of the unscrupulous, unsuccessful soldier of fortune: he may owe something to Iago, but is a good deal older, and without the cold inhuman quality – he recalls, in fact, something between Iago and Bussy d'Ambois. His unillusioned passion for Beatrice-Joanna, his fierce determination to satisfy it in spite of her unconcealed contempt for him, the way in which, when needing him she unbends, he almost falls victim to her cajolery and then pretends that he has really done so, his sardonic self-tormenting joy in the irony of the situation after, are tremendous. Beatrice-Joanna is no less well done. Young, reckless, passionate, she can imagine clearly what she wants, and all things else are merely means or hindrances. Until Piracquo is dead she sees his death as simply the removal of an obstacle, in much the manner of Lady Macbeth and Duncan's. It is only when De Flores reports its accomplishment that she suddenly realizes the thing as murder, and while she is still stricken she is made to learn that De Flores is no passive tool to be used and dropped — and that she is altogether in his power, and must suffer liberties from a man she loathes or lose the other for whose sake she has brought the whole thing on herself. For a while she will not believe the final horror, and confronts him naively with a high moral tone that rouses his sardonic mirth: the whole scene is magnificently done.

The rest of the play falls below — the fourth act rather considerably below — the level of the second and third acts: but even then these two characters carry it off. None of the others are more than lay figures, but De Flores and the girl have few equals in their form of drama, outside Shakespeare.

Unlike some of his neighbours, who appear to have chosen drama as the line of least resistance, Middleton is essentially and instinctively a playwright. His tragic power, at its best, is very notable, and he had a considerable amount of both invention and creative force, as well as more sense of construction than the average. His principal people are generally alive enough — so alive, indeed, that they sometimes make us accept a far-fetched situation. He was not a great poet: one feels, in fact, that his natural temper is rather chilly for great poetry: well as he understands his characters, he never seems to love them. Even with Beatrice-Joanna, though we are made to feel horror and even awe, there is curiously little of the pity that Heywood stirs for the really much more contemptible Mrs. Frankford.

This chill in the man may be the reason why he generally seems to need collaboration. He is one of those people who need another brain to strike the spark for them – a common phenomenon, though the process is not necessarily joint authorship, for Carlyle and his wife, Burns and the old songs, are famous instances, and even Milton seems as a rule to derive his impulse less from direct and personal apprehension of his subject than from considering someone else's handling of it. People like this need someone else to crank the engine, although once started they may run magnificently, and far outgo whatever first inspired them.

ROWLEY, to whom Middleton was several times indebted for this service, may just be mentioned. He did a good deal of work, most of it in collaboration with not only Middleton but Dekker, Fletcher, Massinger, and Webster. As a rule his share would seem to be the comic underplots of low life in London. His own plays, *A Match at Midnight* and *A New Wonder, a Woman never Vexed* have a rough and ready knack of hitting off a situation, and his verse has a certain vigour, if no beauty. But at his best he is no more than a fairly competent journeyman.

JOHN WEBSTER shares Middleton's place on the bridge between the true Elizabethans and the Decadents. As with Middleton, it is his minor work that most looks forward: his greatest is directly in the line of descent through Marlowe, Kyd, and Chapman, and belongs with *Bussy d'Amboise* and *The Spanish Tragedy* rather than *Philaster* or *The Duke of Milan*.

He uses, indeed, a good deal of the old machinery: his greatest two are not actually revenge-plays, but we have the vengeful ghost, the Machiavelian villain, and the elaborate casualty-list. But they are no more derivative than *Hamlet*. Webster had nothing of Shakespeare's range, nor indeed his depth, but he has a greatness that is very much his own. There is horror in the plays, a horror that has the grip of nightmare and its sheer conviction: but it is never *mere* horror. The man was a poet, and a splendid one, with something of the 'lofty, insolent, passionate' vein of Marlowe. The savage darkness has nobility, that comes from a sense of greatness and of pity. His tragedies appal us like Shakespeare's at the things that may befal the human soul, and like Shakespeare's again have that sense in them of the soul's high greatness that nothing else but tragedy can give.

We know almost nothing at all of Webster's life, not even when he was born or when he died. He began to write for the stage about 1601, and produced a good deal, mostly in collaboration. Four plays are certainly his own, however. *Appius and Virginia* is a classical tragedy, not without merit, though it has neither the dignity of Jonson nor the humanity of Shakespeare. *The Devil's Law Case* has some reasonably effective scenes, but on the whole it is pretty second-rate. The others are tremendous: there are things in them that take the spirit like a night storm among great bare stone mountains — only it is a storm of the wind between the worlds.

Both plays come after Shakespeare's work was over. *The White Devil* was printed in 1612 and would seem to have been produced in that year also. *The Duchess of Malfi* may have been produced in 1616, though the printed edition did not appear till 1623. The older play is very much the greater, though it lacks the unearthliness of its successor. But *The*

Duchess has a weaker opening, and its last act is something of an anti-climax to its marvellous fourth. Both plots have that favourite setting, the violent cruelties and suffocating intrigues of the small Italian courts of the Renaissance. *The White Devil*, indeed, is based on actual history, though the other plot is a story of Bandello's. They have as I have said some affinity with the Senecan tragedy of blood, with an insistence on

> 'strange images of death,
> Shadows and shoals that edge eternity.'

Webster has less of the revenge-motif than is common in the type, but he does not need it. Yet in spite of the imminent horror of his plays, they have a superb dark spaciousness that glimmers now and then with royal pity. He has that fiery intense imagination that makes for the sincerity of art: we believe in his people as we believe in Shakespeare's. But we believe in them not because Webster has seen them as human individuals but because he has entered so deeply and passionately the emotions that quicken their being and colour it. It is from this that there spring those bare and marvellous speeches, in words stripped to the bone, like that famous one in the fourth act of *The Duchess of Malfi*, when the Duke of Calabria looks on the dead face of the sister his greedy cold ambition has done to death, and says to Bosola his instrument,

> 'Cover her face: mine eyes dazzle: she died young,'

and is answered,

> 'I think not so: her infelicity
> Seemed to have years too many.'

. . . or touches like her defiant 'I am Duchess of Malfi still' to Bosola's threat at the beginning of her death-scene

The play tells of the young widowed Duchess who has married secretly her Master of the Household. Her brothers, the Duke and the Cardinal, get wind of it when she is with child, and there are some scenes of a fine dramatic tension as their suspicions are aroused. By a curious lapse the play is permitted to drag badly here, for without any explanation, their intervention lags till she has borne three children. Then Ferdinand her brother strikes at last. The scene where the blow falls is admirable. She is chattering in her bed-chamber with her husband and her maid, who knows their secret, and to tease her they steal out while she sits at her glass, and leave her talking, as she thinks, to them. And then she sees in the glass not her husband Antonio, but her brother, who has heard. The sudden change from careless friendly mirth to the stark fear of the discovery and flight is finely handled. But the greatness of the play is in its fourth act, after this, when the Duchess has been captured and imprisoned. Ferdinand tries to shake her reason by fantastic mental torments: she is offered his hand in reconciliation, and finds that she has grasped one dead and severed: he shows her waxen images which she is told are the bodies of her husband and children, and a masque of madmen is let loose in her chamber. Her strangling comes almost as a relief, preluded by the unearthly muted music of the dirge that is sung for her before her living face. The climax is in the terrible low cry of her speech to Bosola, when for a moment her proud courage wavers:

'I know Death hath ten thousand several doors
For men to take their exits; and 'tis found
They go on such strange geometrical hinges
You may open them both ways: any way, for Heaven sake,
So I were out of your whispering.'

There is an abyss of horror in the last phrase, and in Ferdinand's dull muttered words as he enters later to behold his achievement: 'Strangling is a very quiet death.' The whole play is summed in Bosola's last speech,

> 'In what a shadow, or deep pit of darkness
> Doth womanish and fearful mankind live.'

Bosola himself is the greatest of its characters psychologically — a hesitating villain, who forces himself to foul deeds to gain advancement, yet realizes their foulness with an unholy scientific curiosity that is really a twisted and perverted pity. The others have not much individuality, except the Duchess —

> 'on a sudden a clear light
> Presents (her as) a face folded in sorrow' —

but Bosola is finely conceived and not inadequately carried out.

The play as a whole, however, is considerably inferior to the earlier one, which is among the dozen topmost of its kind — indeed, I doubt if one could fill the dozen, even with seven of them Shakespeare's. *The White Devil* has a very complicated plot, moving around the intrigues of the Duke of Brachiano to poison his wife Isabella for the sake of marrying Vittoria his mistress. Isabella's brother, in vengeance for her death, works the apparent downfall of Vittoria; accused of complicity in her own husband's murder, she is brought to trial (a magnificent scene) and sent to a penitentiary. Uncrushed, she lures Brachiano back and gets him to marry her. But he is murdered, and she and her brother Flamineo, their go-between, are put to death. Wrought in with this main action are such episodes as that in which Cornelia finds her son Flamineo has been playing Brachiano's pandar for his own sister, and that in which Flamineo, before her eyes, stabs her young son Horatio, Cornelia's madness, and the shrouding of Horatio to the marvellous dirge. The whole of the action is lurid in the extreme, but its sheer driving force convinces us. Even Brachiano's grotesque ghost in the leather cassock, sprinkling earth on Flamineo, does not make one smile. It is much more even in quality than *The Duchess of Malfi*, and its complex action has remarkable unity: indeed its dramatic power survived and peered through even the astonishingly weak revival of it last winter, when – save for Miss Laura Cowie's competent and beautiful Vittoria – it was worse acted and produced than any play I ever remember to have seen.

The unity and reality come largely from the power of the three main figures. Brachiano is a sort of eidolon of the grosser side of the Renaissance – a full-blooded arrogant bull of a man, but a bull with brains. Flamineo is of the same type as Iago, whose driving power is not as with Brachiano, 'the lust of the flesh, the lust of the eye, and the pride of life,' but a cold pitiless intellect that considers nothing valid but itself. It is a type that, achieved or attempted, one meets fairly often in Elizabethan plays. Iago is the prince of its darkness, but Flamineo comes not too far below him – above, in fact, even Middleton's great De Flores, precisely because the latter is a comprehensible human being, while the others, outside normal humanity, are yet made utterly convincing. Vittoria is done magnificently. She is superb in the sheer brazen effrontery with which she faces her judges and in the arrogant courage of her death, refusing to let her woman precede her into darkness, although

> 'My soul, like to a ship in a black storm,
> Is driven I know not whither.'

As relief, there is some pathos in Isabella and her little son, and the unearthly mourning of Cornelia. The whole play has strange lights through it like a meteor in tempest.

Along with Webster – indeed quite possibly he was his inspiration – one thinks of a man professionally a little senior, CYRIL TOURNEUR. Tourneur's surviving plays, *The Revenger's Tragedy* and *The Atheist's Tragedy* come in 1607 and 1611 respectively. Both are of the same kind as *The White Devil*, but greatly below it, although they have flashes of a gloomy poetry. But their horror has no great dramatic quality. Horrors there are: *The Atheist's Tragedy* makes its Spanish half-namesake look like *Quality Street*. *The Revenger's Tragedy* has a certain coherence, at least, and a grim strength of line in the drawing of the central character Vendice. Its strange and ghastly episodes have a sort of hurtling echo of black poetry, and one or two of the scenes have drama in them, though most of the characters are too merely loathsome for impressiveness. Tourneur was a poet, but rarely: and a dramatist, though more rarely still: a creative psychologist, never.

CHAPTER EIGHT

SHAKESPEARE'S JUNIORS. II

BEAUMONT AND FLETCHER. MASSINGER. FORD.
SHIRLEY. THE FINAL DECADENCE

'D'abord, il a le goût faussé, d'où il résulte qu'il est faible.'
ADOLPHE APPIA, *La Mise en scène du drame wagnérien.*

✱

To turn from Middleton at his best, Tourneur and Webster,
to Beaumont and Fletcher, Massinger and Ford, is like
coming out of a thunderstorm into – a theatre. Though the
older men show plainly enough the onset of the decadence, it
is only in their weaker plays. Their greater hark back to the
tradition of *King Lear* and *Hamlet* rather than forward to
The Maid's Tragedy. But the men who follow them are playwrights rather than dramatists, devotees of the well-made
play with a neat competent action related not too closely to its
characters. The four I have mentioned here are playwrights,
too, of considerable merit, from at any rate the standpoint of
technique. But they are shallower: their tragedy is lavish in
blood, but the blood is thin, with a gruesome inventiveness in
lieu of any real creative vigour, and their comedy is anæmic
under its noise.

In part the change is due to changes in the audience. By
1610 or thereabouts the influence on drama of the universities and the City was giving way to that of a court that
had grown thoroughly rotten under a superficial brilliance.
Elizabeth's held men who were far from scrupulous: but
whatever they did or did not or allowed to be done, they were
generally men at least, and men with brains. And a court
that could also produce Raleigh and Sidney, who were typical

129   I

of a class by no means small, was something more than a mere tangle of intrigues. But in spite of the attractive figures of the two young princes and their charming sister, the Whitehall of James had little to commend it. It kept the surface brilliance, even enhanced it, for the King was a scholar, the Queen fond of display. But – though they revived again on both sides of the Civil War – the traditions that produced the great Elizabethan gentleman must have seemed moribund in 1620.

The typical man of the time felt the older drama too wide and too profound for his own comfort: one sees the same thing in our own thin-brained intellectuals, faced with Shakespeare. Yet if they wanted, instinctively, something a good deal shallower, it still must have a superficial brilliance of poetry about it, for they had not yet reached the state in which men brag about their own stupidity. What they liked was not strong emotion but strong sensation, stuff that would thrill, supply rich spectacle, and an ample fund of familiar jokes upon a single subject. What mattered least was the human interrelations of the characters.

One point in the change is psychologically rather quaint. Mankind has an inherent moral sense, demanding satisfaction: when the other instincts find the moral code of genuinely civilized humanity too burdensome, and jettison it, the need is quieted by the obeying of a new-made and eclectic set of laws: the man who will ruin a girl rather than not gratify a passing physical impulse would spend an hour on the rack rather than walk down Piccadilly in a top hat and brown boots. So the late Jacobean drama combines a general lack of any sense of moral values with an abundance of situations based on a quite artificial point of honour, as that of Amyntor in *The Maid's Tragedy*.

BEAUMONT AND FLETCHER are the leaders of this later group, and very typical, not least in their preference for a new form they label tragi-comedy. 'A tragicomedy is not so called in respect of mirth and killing, but in respect it wants deaths, which is enough to make it no tragedy, yet brings some near it, which is enough to make it no comedy, which must be a representation of familiar people, with such kind of trouble as no life be questioned; so that a god is lawful in this as in a tragedy, and mean people as in a comedy.'

They do in fact rely more on emotional appeal than does comedy proper, which is largely an affair of intellectual perception: but though the emotions of their plays can give rise to – or can at least be adorned by – poetry, they are neither intense enough nor profound enough for the tragic catharsis even when the play does chance to end in death. Their repertory of human types and experiences is very limited, and they stick pretty closely to one single theme, what the publishers' advertisements would call a strong love interest. But the fundamental narrowness of their outlook is somewhat concealed in practice by a freedom of invention in the externals or incidentals of a situation. They make no sort of appeal to the intellect, a fact which partly accounts for their popularity.

I need not say much about the details of their lives, though we know a good deal more of them than of their neighbours. Beaumont was born in 1585 and was an Oxford man: Fletcher, born six years earlier, went to Cambridge. Their collaboration would seem to have begun about 1607 (the probable year of *Antony and Cleopatra*) and though Beaumont's last work appears to come in 1611 and he certainly died in 1616, its influence on Fletcher shows through the nine years he survived his partner. A critic of their own generation said of them that Fletcher had the 'wit' (i.e., invention) and Beaumont the 'judgment' of the partnership.

Their output was considerable, for we have no fewer than fifty-two plays in which one or both of them had a hand at all events. Of these only four were published in Beaumont's lifetime, and during Fletcher's only another four. It is usually considered that *The Woman Hater* and *The Knight of the Burning Pestle* are Beaumont's alone; *Cupid's Revenge, The Scornful Lady, Philaster, The Maid's Tragedy,* and *A King and no King* are joint work, with Beaumont's influence predominant in all except the first two. About fifteen more, the chief of them perhaps being *The Faithful Shepherdess, Monsieur Thomas, Rule a Wife and Have a Wife, Bonduca, Valentinian,* and *The Wild Goose Chase* are written by Fletcher, though with Beaumont's influence still strong in them. In over a score we have Fletcher and another, who in sixteen cases is certainly or probably Massinger, in others Middleton, Rowley, Field, once perhaps Jonson, while in *The Two Noble Kinsmen* it may, though not very probably, have been Shakespeare,[1] and in *Henry VIII* it certainly was, though Fletcher seems to have done most of the actual writing.

It is in the writing, by the way, that we see one of the most conspicuous novelties, a noticeable change in the form of dramatic blank verse, of which they established a new mode that had great influence, colouring, it is thought, even the later work of Shakespeare, whose *Cymbeline* certainly looks like a (rather half-hearted) experiment in their method of

---

[1] Very improbably, I should say. The *versification* in Act I has some rather Shakespearian echoes: but the dramatic handling of speech and action is nowhere in the least like his, though that in *Henry VIII* is decidedly like him at times, even when the actual speeches are not.

handling a story.[1] It certainly influenced Shakespeare's successors, generally for the worse, though with Fletcher himself the innovation is effective, serving his purpose by achieving a more conversational quality of dialogue than is possible, for example, in the sinewy declamatory verse of Chapman. He achieved this end by using a verse that is nearly impossible to declaim – that *has* to be spoken in the tone of ordinary conversation. This effect, not to be too technical about it, is produced in the main by the constant use of an extra syllable at the ends of the lines, muffling the break between them: it is evidently quite conscious and deliberate, for the transition syllable is often a word slightly redundant, and in *The Faithful Shepherdess*, where Fletcher is deliberately lyricizing his subject, he uses a line that is quite firmly endstopped, a verse so unlike his ordinary that one would doubt whether the play were his, if it had not been published in his lifetime. The result of the change is a form midway between verse and prose, and capable, with Fletcher's exquisite ear to guide it, of something of the joint effectiveness of both, though in less competent hands it becomes an unholy sprawling thing with the virtues of neither. The blending of lines, by the way, is a matter purely formal. There is never that strange fierce crushing together of *ideas*, of images interthrust and telescoped by the speed and intensity of the experience beneath them, that you find in the later

[1] This is all that the much-mentioned 'influence' of Beaumont and Fletcher upon Shakespeare really amounts to, except for Fletcher's obvious collaboration in *Henry VIII*. Of the other plays that come with these in dates of writing, *Pericles* is unlikely to have been planned by Shakespeare, as the first two acts are certainly not his. The dramatic treatment of *The Winter's Tale* follows necessarily from its theme and subject, and *The Tempest* is not in the least like Fletcher – or for that matter, anything else of Shakespeare's own.

Shakespeare, especially in the driven soaring verse of the plays between *Othello* and *Coriolanus*. There, the intention is as different as the intensity.

The two friends themselves show certain differences. Beaumont's blank verse, especially in the tragedies, is a good deal nearer the declamatory type, with the natural result that he uses more prose than Fletcher, who seldom needs it. There are differences too in less external points. Beaumont is stronger than his companion on the tragic side, having a keener sense of false notes: for the same reason, he did one capital piece of mock-heroic, which Fletcher avoids, except when he falls into it by accident, and he handles his plots more firmly, partly, perhaps, because they seem to have been more intensely conceived, with some real feeling for the tragic ironies of situation.

Their plots show considerable fecundity of invention – often a virtue of the writer who is otherwise second-rate. As a rule they like a combination of two separate stories, arranged not in the common way of plot and sub-plot, but with at least an attempt to interweave them in the Shakespearian manner, though the union achieved is seldom an organic one. Still, the double plot does make for liveliness of action by ensuring that something is always happening to somebody, and permits of a series of complicated surprises, produced too often by some violent change of character or feeling, whose sole cause is that the surprise requires it. That sufficiently acute critic John Dryden (who in his tragedies was their descendant) remarked with justice that 'they were more concerned with telling what happened to a man than what he was' – to which one may add that they did not always trouble to relate what happened to him to what he was. As is natural, their people tend to follow well-marked types, each clearly labelled so as to be recognized immediately: the wicked king, straining in some fantastic way the loyalty of a devoted subject; the patient Griselda subject who is his counterpart, and believes in the divine right of kings with a thoroughness very acceptable to James VI; the blunt outspoken soldier, generally the hero's friend; the heroine of superhuman virtue; and the vamp of unabashed effrontery. These, of course, are the tragic types, the parents – with a French cross—of the heroicall drama of the Restoration. The comedy ones, where Fletcher's hand is stronger, are no less machine-run, but on the whole nearer to life: the comedies are populated by crowds, all very much alike even in name, of lively, witty, irresponsible young men, rakes by habit and environment, but not bad-hearted nor invariably – though frequently – cads. At their best they are much the type of Tom Jones, though I remember none with anything of Tom's vitality. The women are similar, though the heroines at least are virtuous to the extent of being physically virgin – a point as to which the Elizabethan hero of fiction was rather more particular than ours. They are resourceful, good-humoured, unfastidious, and occasionally witty – the ancestresses of Kate Hardcastle.

Neither Beaumont nor Fletcher was a great dramatic artist. But both were craftsmen of considerable talent. They have a certain amount of intrinsic interest yet, and a much greater historic one, for they were immensely popular, and their influence – indeed some of their plays – lasted into the middle of the nineteenth century. Both, too, had a real poetry, that shows not only in the graceful verse of their more serious dialogue, but in their songs, which are many and enchanting, from snatches of fugitive melody like *Roses, their sharp spines being gone,* or Aspatia's

Lay a garland on my hearse
    Of the dismal yew:
Maidens, willow branches bear;
    Say I died true.

My love was false, but I was firm
    From my hour of birth.
Upon my buried body lie
    Lightly, gentle earth,

to the stately orchestrated music – Fletcher was a magician
with trochaics – of the spring song in *Valentinian*, or in the
same play,

Hear, ye ladies that despise,
    What the cruel Love hath done:
Fear exemples and be wise;
    Fair Calisto was a nun.
Leda, sailing on the stream
    To deceive the hopes of man,
Love accounting but a dream,
    Doted on a silver swan.
        Danae in a brazen tower,
        Where no love was, loved a shower,

and not unlike it, the song of the sea-goddesses in the masque
that celebrates the ominous bridal of Evadne:

Pace out, you watery powers below;
    Let your feet
Like the galleys when they row,
    Even beat.
Let your unknown measures, set
To the still winds, tell to all
That gods are come, immortal, great,
To honour this great nuptial.

Livelier are such things as the war-song in *The Mad Lover* and the gay choruses of *The Spanish Curate*: but it is the slow lute-music of the mournful ones that one remembers.

It is not needful to say much of individual plays, but some are so well-known that they call for mention. Two stand apart from all the rest – Fletcher's *Faithful Shepherdess*, and *The Knight of the Burning Pestle*, which is mostly if not entirely Beaumont's. They are among the best – indeed, are best: but they did not succeed in their own day, from which fact, contrasting their fortune with that of the others, one gathers that they were written for their authors' pleasure, and may also make some deductions about the artistic sincerity of the rest.

The Faithful Shepherdess is one of the loveliest of all the masques: it has less of the pageant element than there is in most of them, and depends for its charm on the sheer grace of writing, on such things as the last – or almost any – speech of the Satyr who plays guardian genius to Clorin its heroine:

> 'Thou divinest, fairest, brightest,
> Thou most powerful maid and whitest,
> Thou most virtuous and most blessed,
> Eyes of stars and golden tressed
> Like Apollo; tell me, sweetest,
> What new service now is meetest
> For the Satyr? Shall I stray
> In the middle air, and stay
> The sailing wrack, or nimbly take
> Hold by the moon, and gently make
> Suit to the pale queen of night
> For a beam to give thee light. . . . '

The sentiment of the whole thing, as usual, has a slightly hectic quality, but in a form so frankly artificial as this it does not matter, though it is a pity that Fletcher felt obliged to drag in the episode of the wanton Cloe, especially as the wantonness of Amaryllis, which is justified by its dramatic point, is already an adequate foil to Amoret and Clorin. But apart from this, the thing as a whole has the airy certainty of Mozart's music and an artistic restraint that Fletcher seldom achieves elsewhere for long at once. It is not surprising that one finds clear echoes of it in *Comus*.

The Knight of the Burning Pestle is quite different, but equally delightful. It is a delicious piece of sheer buffoonery — a skit on the popular adventure-drama of the *Four Prentices of London* type, with a dash of citizen humour-comedy. A worthy cit takes his wife and his pet apprentice, Ralph, to see the edifying drama of the merchant Venturewell, his daughters and his prentices. But the prologue does not please: Master Citizen leaps on the stage to argue about it, and demands, 'I will have a play about a grocer, and he shall do admirable things.' His lady below chips in with 'Let him kill a lion with a pestle, husband, let him kill a lion with a pestle!' and makes her way on to the stage herself. . . .

'*Wife.* By your leave, gentlemen all; I'm something troublesome: I'm a stranger here; I was never at one of these plays, as they say, before, but I should have seen *Jane Shore* once; and my husband hath promised me, any time this twelvemonth, to carry me to *The Bold Beauchamps*, but in truth he did not. I pray you, bear with me.

Citizen. Boy, let my wife and me have a couple of stools and then begin; and let the grocer do rare things.

(*Stools are brought.*)

Speaker of Prologue. But, sir, we have never a boy to play him: every one hath a part already.

Wife. Husband, husband, for God's sake, let Ralph play him! Beshrew me if I do not think he will go beyond them all.

Citizen. Well remembered, wife. Come, Ralph. I'll tell you, gentlemen, let them but lend him a suit of reparel and necessaries. . . .

(*Ralph comes on the stage.*)

Wife. I pray you, youth, let him have a suit of reparel. I'll be sworn, gentlemen, my husband tells you true: he will act sometimes, at our house, that all the neighbours cry out on him; he will fetch you up a couraging part so in the garret, that we are all as feared, I warrant you, that we quake again We'll fear our children with him: if they be never so unruly, do but cry, "Ralph comes! Ralph comes!" and they'll be as quiet as lambs. Hold up thy head, Ralph: show the gentlemen what thou canst do: speak a huffing part: I warrant you, the gentlemen will accept it.

Citizen. Do, Ralph, do.

Ralph. "By heaven, methinks it were an easy leap
    To pluck bright honour from the pale-faced
      moon;
    Or dive into the bottom of the sea
    Where never fathom-line touched any ground,
    And pluck up drowned honour from the lake of
      hell." [1]

Citizen. How say you, gentlemen, is it not as I told you?

Wife. Nay, gentlemen, he hath played before, my husband says, Mucedorus, before the wardens of our company.

[1] *Henry IV*, Part I – slightly enriched!

Citizen. Ay, and he should have played Jeronimo with a shoemaker, for a wager.

Speaker of Prologue. He shall have a suit of apparel, if he will go in.'

The rest is a glorious mixture – the original play, itself an admirable piece of parody, interpolations by Ralph, as a sort of cross between Hudibras and Don Quixote, and a running fire of comment from Ralph's master and mistress, to the tribulation of the protesting players. In the middle of a touching scene the lady has a sudden brain-wave:

'Ralph, I would have thee call all the youths together in battle-ray, with drums and guns and flags, and march to Mile-End in pompous fashion, and there exhort your soldiers to be merry and wise, and to keep their beards from burning, Ralph; and then skirmish, and let your flags fly, and cry "Kill, kill, kill!" My husband shall lend you his jerkin, Ralph, and there's a scarf; for the rest, the house shall furnish you, and we'll pay for't. Do it bravely, Ralph, and think before whom you perform, and what person you represent.'

Which is duly done, with appropriate official rhetoric, wickedly like the real thing even to-day. Beaumont, on his own confession, wrote the play in a week, and the speed and gusto of the writing inform it all.

None of their serious work compares with these by-products of their muse. Even *Philaster* and *The Maid's Tragedy* are rather effective plays than great drama. Both held the stage for long, and were very popular, largely, no doubt, on account of the splendid chances they give the heroine, for all the great actresses of the eighteenth century delighted in Bellario and Evadne. The latter, indeed, has one scene at least with some real power in it – that in which her

A King and no King also is fairly effective, and there is a
certain vigour about the vainglorious and passionate Arbaces,
who unfortunately falls in love with the lady whom everyone
believes his sister. Of course she is really nothing of the kind,
and after five acts of violent emotions they are married off
most respectably. There is some humour in the braggart
Bessus, a part on the lines of Bobadil or Parolles. *Bonduca*
(Boadicea) has been praised, though it seems to me, for the
most part, rather chilly rant. *Valentinian*, which is all
Fletcher's, rehashes elements from the other plays, with a
violent volte-face on the hero's part to enliven – and ruin –
the last act: its chief claim to notice is the remarkable number
of very lovely songs. *The Bloody Brother* and *Thierry and
Theodoret* – both partly Massinger's – are much of the same
kind. The latter is a variant of the Jephtha's Daughter
motif: the virtuous Thierry is duped by his wicked mother
and brother into a vow to sacrifice the first living thing he
meets, which they contrive shall be his wife Ordella. Lamb
praises highly the scene between them when Ordella realizes
the truth and offers to submit: and there is a remote and
frigid grace about the writing. But the entire lack of life in
the characters or of the faintest attempt at plausibility in the
action makes the quality even of this quite non-dramatic, and
the rest of the play is unmitigated pasteboard. *The Two Noble
Kinsmen*, on the story of Chaucer's *Knight's Tale*, found its
way into the Shakespearian apocrypha. That it should do so
shows how long it took our critics to acquire any perception
of difference (let alone quality) in *dramatic* technique, dis-
tinguished from poetic. It is just possible that Shakespeare
may have touched some speeches, or that they incorporate
scrap-work of his: but that he should have had anything to do
with it as a *play* is as likely as that Mr. Shaw wrote part of

Deirdre of the Sorrows. It is probable, or even certain, that Shakespeare did have something to do with *Henry VIII* — pageant, but admirable pageant, with an underlying theme, to unify it, that was certainly much in Shakespeare's mind about that time. Not much of the actual writing can be his: it is good, but quite unlike his kind of goodness. But the outline, the dramatic handling, of Katharine's trial — though not the dialogue itself of it — is considerably more in his manner than in Fletcher's.

The comedies, for the most part, are very poor. Perhaps *The Scornful Lady* is the best of them. Some of the scenes in the duel of wits between Loveless and the Lady are rather amusing, but they are too long-drawn-out. And the conclusion shows a characteristic weakness of the writer's: an artist is perfectly entitled, if he choose, to draw a cad, but it is fatal if he does not know him for one. Martha, the Lady's young sister, takes Welford's part with generous and plucky sympathy when she believes him to be a woman wronged by Loveless: he uses the opportunity so gained to seduce her, and brags of it to the whole house next morning: and the author appears to consider the business a good joke. *The Woman Hater* — Beaumont's — has a main plot as nearly neglible as may be, though there is some mild fun in the farcical sub-plot where the glutton Lazarillo, in desperate quest for a taste of the Duke's rare fish, is half-overheard by spies who translate his talk into a plot of murder, and lands in prison. *The Wild Goose Chase* is the successful pursuit of a misogynistic youth by the lady he has sworn never to marry. Played at speed it might be mildly if not excessively amusing. It is odd, by the way, that Mr. Shaw's commentators insist on finding his sources exclusively in Ibsen and Nietzsche, for Oriana is Ann Whitefield in a farthingale. *Monsieur Thomas* has a promising theme, in the difficulties of a travelled youth who has to convince, simultaneously, his father that he is a rake and his lady-love that he is most respectable. The idea is admirable in its way, but the opportunities are not used, and the play is as dull as an American version of a machine-made Palais Royal farce. Fletcher adopted the Jonsonian humour-comedy in *The Nice Valour* and *The Humorous Lieutenant*, and the Shakespearian romantic comedy in *The Spanish Curate*: but there is a flavour of mass-production in them all.

John Ford and PHILIP MASSINGER are both of the disciple-ship of Fletcher. Ford has the faults, exaggerated, and touches, though only touches, of the poetry. Massinger, though less of a poet than Ford, and much less than Fletcher, is a better dramatist than either of his masters, and suffers least from the pasteboard-and-tinsel staginess of the school. Possibly one reason for this is that he had a firmer, more clear-sighted sense of conduct. The conduct itself, to be sure, has often no more than an interest of the theatre – though to be just, it generally has that – but the values themselves have enough reality to give at least a temporary life to the situations in his plays.

He was born in 1583, the son of a poor gentleman in the service of Lord Pembroke. He was an Oxford man, going down about 1609, and we know that he was writing plays in 1614, though the earliest that has survived is *The Virgin Martyr*, written with Dekker somewhat later than this – about the time, that is, of Shakespeare's death. He died in 1640, having written well over thirty plays, of which eighteen are extant. Their merit varies from a really fine comedy, rather like Molière in handling and conception, *A New Way to Pay Old Debts*, down to some very poor stuff indeed: and their kinds

are nearly as various as their merits. After the really fine –
one could say great – play I have mentioned come the
effective tragi-comedy of *The Maid of Honour*; a pleasant
romantic comedy, *The Great Duke of Florence*; and a tragedy,
The Duke of Milan, which is the best serious play of the
whole school. *The Roman Actor* is a tolerable classical
tragedy, *The City Madam* citizen-comedy of the Dekker
type, amusing in parts. *The Virgin Martyr* probably owes
its best thing, the graceful figure of St. Dorothy its heroine,
to Dekker, and most of the rest of it is tedious or worse. None
of the others call for any mention.

Of the four plays mentioned above as chief, all but *A New
Way* are frankly modelled on the work of Beaumont and
Fletcher, with the latter of whom their writer often collaborated. In all of them he surpasses, from the dramatic standpoint, his two masters. As a poet, of course, he is not within
a mile of Fletcher, though he wrote a sound and competent
blank verse, that at its best is really dignified. But he has a
firmer intellectual quality: it would be absurd to speak of him
as a great thinker, but he seems to have been an intelligent
man who observed life thoughtfully and reflected, if not
profoundly, on what he saw. It is this, perhaps, that makes
for his excellent construction: in the putting together of a
play he is much superior to many greater men, and evidently
had learned a lot from Shakespeare. He has the knack of
opening a play excellently. Though he never shows anything like the great imaginative strokes of Shakespeare's
openings, he uses the expository talk of his characters very
deftly and economically, and sometimes achieves something
more than that, as in the first scene of *The Duke of Milan*,
with the atmosphere of fey apprehensive happiness he contrives to cast over the festivities of the Duchess' birthday –

K

rejoicings that are steadily undermined, first by the smothered enmity of her sister-in-law, and then by the arrival of the successive couriers who bring the news of the defeat at Pavia. The final acts, unfortunately, are seldom as good as the beginnings – very often because he tried to be too tidy, to tie off all his threads symmetrically, with a proper distribution of poetic justice. As happens rather often to dramatists with a strong sense of general form, he is weak in psychology; indeed, the most part of his folk are puppets, though it is only fair to add that they are generally the kind of puppets good acting could give life. His stock-in-trade consists as a rule of serious moral purpose and a good and well-ordered action to reveal it: and the characters must go where they are put. One feels that instead of getting into them, seeing through their eyes, feeling with their emotions, he sits above manipulating. He is always a spectator of his creations, though a spectator whose imagination can be stirred by them, so that he sometimes does achieve intensity of a simple and uncomplex tragic passion, although he cannot handle disastrous internal conflicts of the soul.

It is this disability that goes some way to spoil *The Maid of Honour*. There is something almost naive in the way in which Bertoldo falls victim to the wiles of Aurelia, though he is bound by every tie of honour, love, and gratitude to Camiola. It is not of course impossible in itself that he might have fallen: but we do not in the least believe in him as we see him do it. In spite of this flaw, the play is rather attractive, at any rate among its neighbours of the time. When Adorni, Camiola's rejected lover, sacrifices himself, without fuss or heroics, to save the man she does love, his abnegation is made real, not stagey. Camiola herself, though like all Massinger's women she is done from the outside, is both consistent and on the whole attractive, and the final scene, where she shames her false lover into repentance, and passes, at the full of her triumph, from the glitter of the court into a nunnery, is both effective and unusual. The play suffers badly from its pervasion by the conventional fop Sylli: but it is probable that it would act.

It has been set at the top of Massinger's work, for the sake of Camiola: but though she is certainly the most attractive of his women, one cannot call her a great dramatic figure. None of them are that. Meg Overreach in *A New Way*, Lidia in *The Great Duke of Florence*, are pleasant enough but very colourless, and the rest have the cheapness of conception that mars Beaumont and Fletcher. The bad ones, like Beaumelle in *The Fatal Dowry*, are meant as great sirens like Vittoria Corombona, but resemble more nearly the vamps of Hollywood. This is true of as competent and effective a play as *The Duke of Milan*, which a different Marcelia might have made a great one.

Even as it is, parts of it have power: and it is made effective by its speed and concentration. There is something of the real colour of the Italian Renaissance in Sforza, and even in Francisco. It is indeed the best serious play of the group, far better than *Philaster* or *The Maid's Tragedy*, both as a stage-play and in the general quality of its imagination. Sforza, the Duke, who loves his Duchess with the wolfish egoistic passion that so often goes for love in these plays, has backed the wrong side in the strife between France and the Emperor, and is forced to surrender to the Emperor's discretion, to save Milan from sack by the Imperial troops. Unsure of returning alive, he leaves with his brother-in-law and favourite Francisco a written commission of authority to kill the Duchess in the event of his own death. Francisco has a vendetta against the lady because – as we do not learn till a good deal later – Sforza has seduced his sister under promise of marriage, then thrown her over for Marcelia. So he attempts, at first, revenge in kind, making love to Marcelia, and when he is rejected, showing her the commission. He succeeds in rousing her to anger with Sforza, but she declines to revenge herself in the manner he has suggested. So aided by his wife, who hates her, he stirs the Duke's jealousy, Iago-fashion, and Marcelia plays into his hands by her coldness to her husband on his return, and by informing him, to pay him out for the commission, that she loves Francisco. Sforza, in a rage of agony, stabs her at once, and there is a fantastic but effective close where he dies kissing the poisoned lips of her dead body, which Francisco has painted to a semblance of returning life. The play just misses greatness: but it has a straightforward effective vigour, a directness and economy of structure, that give it admirable acting quality. Taken at the right pace it would play much better than it reads: and it reads by no means badly, so long as one does not remember *The White Devil*.

The Great Duke of Florence has a good deal of the same virtues. It is romantic comedy, with a lively and well-managed plot of cross-purposes, just serious enough to hold our interest, and is remarkable among its group for the pleasantness of its characters. They are all drawn slightly enough, but the conception of them is noticeably free from the hectic morbidity that was distressingly frequent as the first quarter of the century drew to its close. It is not great drama, but a very competent and lively stage-play.

There is, however, one play in which Massinger achieves something uncommonly like greatness. This is the excellent comedy, *A New Way to Pay Old Debts*. It is unlike the rest, in having no affinity to the typical Beaumont and Fletcher model. Rather it derives from the grim vigorous Jonsonian comedy, such as *The Alchemist*. It lacks the almost violent verve of that, but it has plenty, and the construction is both neat and deft. Further, though Massinger has less power than some of his neighbours to penetrate the secret places of the heart (whether its temple or its drainage system) he does create here one great dramatic character in the usurer Sir Giles Overreach, who may stand beside, and not too far below, Volpone or Harpagon. It is a study of the remorseless capitalist, to whom the acquiring of money – the acquisition rather than the actual money – is the mainspring of his life, with as second to it the desire to found a family, to marry his daughter and heiress to Lord Lovel, so that his grandson shall be a nobleman. The action of the play is the plot to ruin him, carried out by the nephew he has ruined and his own creature Marrall, a strange Dickensian personage, nearly as vivid as his master. Overreach treats him with a cynical offhandedness, as a mere catspaw: and Marrall knows it, and hating him, bides his time. These two are the play's greatest element; none of the others matter very much, though at the same time, with much addition to its dramatic effectiveness, some of them are more 'sympathetic' than Jonson's characters. The stuff is handled with a really fine sense of the stage, and it is not surprising that it held the theatre until the middle of last century.

Massinger brings the towering poetries of the earlier men to prose: but it is an effective prose, if artificial. He does not carry us beyond ourselves, but his better plays would certainly hold an audience. *The Maid of Honour*, even *The Duke of Milan*, do not purge our souls with pity and terror. I think I could eat chocolates even in *The Duke*, which would be unlikely in even a mediocre version of *Othello*. But it would need a very bad production to make it bore me – and it would survive a bad producer much more comfortably than the fundamentally far greater work of Chapman, perhaps even of Webster. One could recommend it to the Renaissance Theatre.

The last name of note on the roll of the Jacobeans is JOHN FORD, a writer who in the past has been remarkably over-praised – surprisingly by Lamb and much more comprehensibly by Swinburne, who suffering himself from Ford's defects, was the less likely to be troubled by them. He is in the fullest Beaumont and Fletcher tradition, absorbing and exaggerating all its worst faults of staginess and lack of emotional logic, and the falsetto of extravagance they take for power. It is this last that damns him, rather than any madness of his matter. The fantastic horrors of *'Tis Pity She's a Whore* are not really, in themselves, more lurid than Tourneur or Webster: but even Tourneur, for all his half-crazy vehemence, has still a sort of mad masculinity about him. Ford makes one think rather of Reginald Bunthorne: he is the dapper shrill-voiced little poet whose well-advertised vices are less the result of uncontrollable desire than of a wish to shock his audience in a fresh place. He belongs with the green carnation gentry of the 'nineties, and like the still popular heirs of that forgotten school, has the obsession with the unwholesome side of sex that is one of the regular marks of defective virility. Like the 'nineties, too, and like his immediate masters, he is not without a colour of poetic fancy; and more than Beaumont and Fletcher and the average though not the best of Massinger, he has that intensity of expression that looks like passion till you put it by the real thing.

We know little of him, though one or two of the things we do are rather odd. He was probably born about the middle of the fifteen-eighties, of a good Devon family, and wrote his plays 'because he wanted to,' and not from any need to write for money. His dramatic career lasted some thirty years, but very little work of his survives, and it does not tempt one greatly to regret what is lost. He is known to have collaborated with Dekker in *The Witch of Edmonton* and *The Sun's Darling*, and with Webster in a lost crime-piece, *A Late Murder of the Son upon the Mother*, which must have been a fairly lurid business. The surviving plays that are probably all his are *Perkin Warbeck*, *Love's Sacrifice*, *The Broken Heart*, *'Tis Pity She's a Whore*, *The Fancies Chaste and Noble*, *The Lady's Trial*, and *The Lover's Melancholy*.

The last three are pretty negligible. *Perkin Warbeck* is a chronicle-play, clearly arranged and competent, but chilly. Of the remaining three *'Tis Pity* is traditionally praised. The theme of the incestuous loves of Giovanni and his sister Annabella might have been made tragic enough, and Annabella a Jacobean Phèdre. In point of fact, though there are speeches of some intensity, the note of the whole is curiously vulgar. The atmosphere is less that of suffocating tragic intrigue than of a giggling calf-love between a furtive schoolboy and an underbred 'young lady' from Miss Pinkerton's. When Giovanni rushes in with Annabella's bleeding heart upon his dagger the effect is as near tragedy as if it were a pound of sausages. Indeed the sausages would be more tragic, for they might suggest the spoiling of someone's breakfast! Perhaps it is because the lovers have so little dignity. They fall, in the first place, rather from spinelessness than from consuming passion; they talk to each other like Edwin and Angelina in a *Punch* of the eighteen-seventies; and neither

they nor – more fatally still – the author, seems aware that
the means they use to cover their intrigue are merely contemptible. It is interesting to note that the editor of the
Mermaid Ford (published in the eighteen-nineties) talks of
the fineness of Ford's moral perception.

The Broken Heart is a much better thing. It has in fact a
sort of Tchekhovian atmosphere of vague heartbreak all
round, among people whose spiritual temperatures appear
subnormal – where, in a phrase from itself, 'one sings
another's knell.' Its most famous scene, Calantha dancing
on as one messenger after another brings news of death, is
effective for a moment if one does not stop to think about it.
But there is no particular reason why she should go on dancing: and we realize very soon, and chillingly, that she is doing
it not out of gallant self-control, nor forced by any ironic
compulsion of necessity, but simply to provide a new stage
thrill. The final episode, where she weds the dead Ithocles,
has an effectiveness, if one can keep one's mind on the right
artificial plane. But none of the people or their deeds enforce
belief. To apply my recent test of tragedy, I could eat
chocolate during any act of it – if I had not gone home to bed
by about the third.

Love's Sacrifice, like *'Tis Pity*, has a theme with fine
dramatic possibilities. One could imagine an excellently
sardonic play on a man's recoil when his wooing of his friend's
wife proves successful. What one gets is a Jacobean *The
Green Hat*. The loves of the two, handled with Ford's
adolescent feverishness, are unconvincing to begin with: and
when, being murdered by the lady's husband before they have
time to *couronner leur flamme*, as by this time apparently they
both intend, they are solemnly held up as miracles of chastity,
the result is something very Arlenesque. One observes that

Mr. Havelock Ellis calls Ford modern: and it is certainly true that he has much the same thin-blooded feverishness, with a strong tendency to the falsetto, that mark the school that since 1888 or so has claimed the adjective, and which seems to be the final phase of the period from which we are just reacting, from Wordsworth and Shelley to Mr. Aldous Huxley and Mr. Lawrence. Mr. Ellis also remarks, much more surprisingly, that Ford shows insight in the drawing of his women. We are not told where, and I have not been able to discover it. They are not so much incredible as non-existent, unless perhaps Annabella, who might be Lydia Bennet in less reputable circumstances. But Ford's verse has a sort of frigid grace about it: the chaos of the decasyllable had not descended on him. And he achieves one musical song in *The Broken Heart.*

The last of the group to be born under Elizabeth is JAMES SHIRLEY, who saw light in the year 1596. He wrote a good deal, but he lives less as a dramatist than in virtue of one splendid sombre lyric –

> 'The glories of our blood and state
> Are shadows, not substantial things' –

from *The Contention of Ajax and Ulysses.* His work is on the Beaumont and Fletcher tradition, his first play coming in 1625. There are touches of poetry in him and some sense of stagecraft, and he is about the last to have any ear for dramatic blank verse. His best tragedy is *The Cardinal,* his best comedy *The Lady of Pleasure.* But neither matters much except historically.

The same tradition runs through a large group of minors –

Randolph, Suckling, Davenant, Browne, Nabbes, Cokane, Marmion, and so on: there are quite a lot of them. Its weak points were growing, such merits as it had were dying out: the spark of poetry that had illumined it was quenched for good in the chaotic deadness of its verse. When the theatres closed in 1642, 'for the duration of the war,' the English drama, with barely sixty years of life behind it, was already come upon its dotage, in a doddering and uncomely senility that is pitiful after the fiery youth of Marlowe and the vivid manhood of the quarter-century between 1590 and the death of Shakespeare. There is a flicker of recovery in the dialogue at least of a few of the mechanical comedies of the Restoration, the glittering liveliness of Sheridan, and the neat quick wit of Goldsmith and some of the eighteenth-century libretti Mr. Playfair has so pleasantly revived for us. But then, apparently, the torch went out, to dwell in darkness till there blew into it a spark from Norway, and another kindled in the Abbey Theatre.

In the last thirty years we have again a drama, and there are abundant signs that in spite of much negligible rubbish, these thirty years were only a beginning. Perhaps for that reason we are less likely to lose our heads over Shakespeare's contemporaries, and the almost hysterical praise of our fathers leaves us bewildered, forgetting that in a time when your 'modern' critic scoffed at the eighteenth century as our young 'moderns' do at the Victorians and the eighteenth-century 'moderns' at the Elizabethans, such superlatives were much what one might expect. And it is amusing to see critics of our own day inverting this particular enthusiasm, and attempting to dazzle us by the assurance that of course Shakespeare couldn't write a play.

There is no reason why we should exaggerate, or yelp our

admiration or disgust. A great part of Elizabethan drama, like
a great part of any other age's drama, is rubbish. A good deal
more of it is rather dead. Yet there remains a body of fine
imaginative work, at the best of it white-hot with fiery
energy, deep-reaching and far-reaching, with a strong noble
beauty and profound humanity. The more one reads it, the
more one realizes, even a shade unwillingly, how Shakespeare
towers, all ways, above his neighbours, his colossal supremacy
over even Webster, even the best of Jonson, Dekker, Marlowe, Middleton, Heywood. Yet even so, his work is so
immeasurable that their best can yet remain a very great one.
There is one glory of the sun and another of the stars. One
may admit, fully, the sun's is greater, and yet find a rich
pleasure in Orion.

CHAPTER NINE

THE ELIZABETHAN PLAY ON THE MODERN STAGE

'This may seem a presumptuous order.'
GEORGE GASCOIGNE, *Certain Notes of Instruction.*

✻

MY purpose in this chapter is not an historical sketch of the various Elizabethan revivals. What I am trying to do is merely to offer a few practical suggestions to the producer, particularly to the amateur producer, for Elizabethan drama, especially tragic, 'comes through' uncommonly well in the hands of amateurs, provided only they can speak its verse. Comedy of the intellectual or artificial types, of Shaw or Sheridan, tragedy of the inarticulate or dreamily decorative kind, all need professional technique, and need it badly: few amateurs can make a good job of *The School for Scandal*, though every year some hundreds of them try. But what the Elizabethan tragedy most needs is a freshness and sincerity of the imagination – precisely the quality in which good amateurs outstrip all but the best professionals. One must know, of course, such elementary points of technique as how to avoid 'blocking' another player, which knee to go down on in a curtsey to the right or left. But a very little of the mechanic side of acting goes a long way: a producer with a pictorial eye can supply most of it. What matters is the spirit and the speech, and next to these, and hardly less important in practice, speed.

To go through the practical points in detail, one of the first is the preparation of the play itself. As a rule I strongly object to 'revising' any literature that is worth anything at all – certainly to pulling it about as our fathers did. Astonishing as it would seem to Sir Henry Irving, or even to the still extant Mr. Baynton, Shakespeare did know how to put a play together. So did some other men of his contemporaries, and cursed be he who moves the bones of their work. Nevertheless, it is not necessary to be fanatical. In many of the plot-and-sub-plot plays – *The Changeling* and *The Honest Whore* are obvious cases – the two sides of the play are so entirely separable, and so very far apart in quality, that from any standpoint but the pure historical the excision of the sub-plot is quite justified. In *The Honest Whore* indeed, to drop the sub-plot would permit the telescoping of its two parts, so as to make one action of Bellafront's conversion and its sardonic sequel, with obvious advantages. Again, some of the plays may perhaps need shortening to be manageable, though – being used to the Old Vic – I deprecate as strongly as possible mere cutting for cutting's sake. Yet there are stretches of mechanical low-comedy that would excellently bear the scissors: and there is, too, the question of expurgation. To the very young, of course, the mere word is anathema. But one may accept a good deal of broadness in one's humour, yet fail to see humour in dirt for dirt's sake. Of course there is real dramatic value in, for example, the syphilitic jesting of Lucio and his friends in *Measure for Measure*. It is neither pleasant nor humorous, nor is it meant to be. It is meant to draw Vienna for us, and it does. To cut it is to injure the dramatic structure of the play, as cutting Pandarus ruins *Troilus and Cressida*. And if anyone wants to bowdlerize Doll Tearsheet, or the last act of *Eastward Ho*, I will gladly lend a hand with the tar and feathers. But also, if anyone feels inclined to disinfect the 'wit' of Middleton's sub-plots by a judicious use of the blue pencil, I am no less ready to call

him entirely right. There are certain stock jests, mechanic-
ally repeated, that were the Elizabethan mother-in-law and
kipper jokes. They are no funnier, and much more unpleasant, and I see no reason why they should be sacrosanct. The
points to be considered are (*a*) are they dramatically necessary? (*b*) are they funny? If they are neither, they can well
be spared. But apart from such cuts as may be required for
the sake of time or of the relevant decencies, it is a mistake to
rearrange the plays. Their dramatic idiom, with its quick
shift of scene, may be unfamiliar, though it is less so if one is
used to the cinematograph. But on the stage it 'gets across'
very well, *if* the stage is so equipped as to allow it.

The said equipment need not be very complex. There is
no occasion to be too archæological: if one is to have the
apron platform, the galleried open theatre, one may as well
let the audience sit on the stage and smoke, and play by daylight. But there are one or two essentials. One is to remember that it is necessary, for the sake of speed, to have as little
scenery as possible, to concentrate on a background that
does not call attention to itself when the scene is localized,
that provides a suitable and inconspicuous frame when it is
not, and add to it only such furniture as may be necessary.
The traditional placard – LONDON, DALMATIA, A WOOD,
ARETHUSA'S CHAMBER – may be hung up if you think it is
required. Perhaps the best setting, especially for amateurs, is
plain curtains, of black velvet for a tragedy, of some colour,
not too bright, for comedy. The black velvet, with plentiful
heavy folds, has a sombre richness, and throws up splendidly
colour and gesture. It is equally good, by the way, for many
kinds of fantastic or artificial comedy: I have seen the *School
for Scandal* played against it, and the effect of powdered wigs

and bright brocades, relieved thus, was enchanting. Tapestry, painted on harding, will be effective in some things, but it should be kept quite unobtrusive.

A front curtain may or may not be used. It depends a good deal on whether the audience are likely to accept the appearance of the Third Soldier or the Second Serving-man to carry stools and tree-stumps on and off between the scenes. In the Birkbeck Elizabethan plays it has always been omitted, and the audience seemed to get used to the convention. I do not think it is very material with a curtain setting, though if there is to be any change of scene – even backcloth – as well as of accessories, it is better perhaps that there should be one.

The backcloth itself must be made to part and draw up, not only for entrances, but to drape an alcove that may serve as rear stage. Often the action demands this, and sometimes when not strictly necessary it can be used with much decorative effect, say to frame and canopy a throne or altar.

There is of course no reason why one should restrict oneself to curtains. Provided the sets are simple, easily changed, and *always background*, they may have much value, not only decorative but 'atmospheric.' They should aim rather at suggesting a place than representing it, but when they do that well, as in some of Mr. Garside's recent sets for the Old Vic, they may have immense dramatic value. One does not forget Desdemona's high scarlet bed against the shadows, the ominous brazier lighting Leontes' jealousy, the mooncast shadows of *Midsummer Night's Dream*, or the sweep of the stone stairs in the most effective set for *Macbeth* that I remember. The best plan, probably, is that used by Lovat Fraser in *The Beggar's Opera* and now regularly (and wisely) by many other designers – a simple permanent set, with backcloths and accessories, such as seats and tables, that can be *swiftly* moved to alter it. But always, always, it should be no picture, but a frame for the action of the figures grouped within it.

One of the most serious shortcomings of the Elizabethan stage, as of every other till the last half-century, was the practical impossibility of light effects. We should be foolish to deny ourselves their help – the strong emotional as well as decorative quality of brightness or gloom, green moonlight or the orange glow of torches, or such more complex devices as the setting of certain figures in relief.[1] If they could not use these at the Globe there is no doubt whatever that they would have liked to. Shakespeare, when he wrote, most obviously saw his action lighted – take any of the tragedies for instance – and must have sorrowed for the need that had them played eventually in the haphazard luck of British daylight. Again the essential point is not to obtrude it. It should supplement the imaginative quality of the play, not get in front of it. Within these limits, there are admirable chances, and no reason for refusing to accept them. The amateur, of course, must cut his coat according to his cloth. He may have oil-lamps. Even if he has, I think he is wise to attempt at least such modulation as may indicate darkness when the play requires it. To light alike the second act of *Macbeth* and the banquet scene would try a modern audience too far. To the amateur who has a stage with some command of electric lighting (and one should be as much a part of every

---

[1] Anyone who saw Sir Barry Jackson's production of *The Immortal Hour* will recall a most beautiful instance of this in the cottage scene. The effect so caught the imagination of one member of the audience that she had no peace of mind until she had attempted to reproduce it in her own medium – which happened to be narrative prose!

school or college as the gymnasium or the laboratory) I would suggest that the bulbs for the full light should be yellow – a true yellow, not lemon. The coloured bulbs are no more expensive than the plain: or if the company are in temporary quarters, thin *cheap* Japanese silk (good silk is much too thick) tied over them, will do. Long before coloured bulbs were procurable I used it for the 100w. bulb in my own sitting-room. It makes an extraordinary difference to the quality of the colours, and is kinder to make-up in a small theatre.

Apart from lighting, the main purely decorative element, besides grouping and movement, is the costume. There the producer has every justification for letting himself go, to the full extent financially possible. Elizabethan costume may have been uncomfortable to live in, but few periods have been more arrogantly decorative. I say Elizabethan: and I mean it. The Elizabethan playwright filled all that he created with the peculiar and characteristic temper of the time, and the dress of that time is as much the outcome of that temper as the diction. The only real exception would be the Roman plays, or at least some of them. Jonson's at least, *Coriolanus*, *Julius Cæsar*, are evidently meant to have a Roman atmosphere. In *Antony and Cleopatra*, too, however much Renaissance there is in it, a great part of the theme under the subject is seen in terms of the clash between Rome and the East: and the décor, costume included, should help the stress on the antithesis. But these are exceptional. Even the usual run of the 'histories' are better dressed as in the period of their authors. I have seen *Edward II* so done, and it was done rightly. In the 'fancy' histories – *Macbeth* or *Hamlet*, say – to rig these thoroughly Renaissance folk in the garments of

L

the sagas is like putting a farthingale on Hedda Gabler. The
Old Vic has recently (quite unregarded by the critics) dressed
Hamlet properly, and the result more than vindicated common sense against the traditional mixture of ninth and fourteenth century, or such journalese experiments as the putting
of the Prince of Denmark in plus fours.[1]

There is no reason, except a possible financial one, why the
producer should quarrel with the limitation. The professional
producer can spend on dress what the simplicity of his scene
has saved him: and may remember that furniture brocade
can be most gorgeous. Let him not fear colour, especially
deep red and orange: and there ought to be a fair amount of
black, both silk and velvet, and of metal and gems that catch
the light and gleam. It is difficult to make a Renaissance
court too splendid. Stage lighting is very kind to conflicting
colour, but it ought not to be tried too far. I remember (in a
much-advertised professional performance) a Viola in crude
blotting-paper pink playing opposite to a peach-coloured
Orsino: and it did not assist one's sense of the play's poetry.
And when Horatio in jade-green makes love to Bellimperia
in sage-colour, more teeth than Balthasar's will be on edge.

To the amateur I may add advice more detailed. *His*
costumes will probably be hired. If they are, let him appoint
some competent person as sartorial editor to the whole cast.
It is extraordinary how six-penn'orth of safety-pins can
improve the fit, set, and apparent freshness of even the most
dilapidated hireling. And there are two points in especial
that call for very careful notice, for they make an enormous
difference to the visual impression of a play. One is the ruffs.

---

[1] If we *are* going to 'modernize,' I should rather like to see *Julius
Cæsar* set in the costume of 1848. Brutus and his wife are so exactly what
we mean when we say 'Victorian,' that it would fit well enough.

The hired ruff is a non-committal business: 'like the barber's stool, it fits every man.' But it fits few of them becomingly unless it is very carefully adjusted. Agamemnon would look effeminate if you put him into a loose collar that was low, but closed in front: it would be interesting to know how much the popular estimate of the clergy has been unconsciously biassed by their neck-gear. The ruffs must fit. And they ought to be tilted at the proper angle. The narrow ruff, sewn on the collar, is easiest to deal with: if it fits pretty close it is all right. The larger ones, made separate, must rise at the back: it may not be easy, but it has to be contrived somehow. And – in italics – *it must never flop.* The equivalent, in the woman's case, is wire. Their head-dresses, their deep lace collars, are full of wire, which generally arrives shapeless. The beauty, and the historic atmosphere of the whole costume, depend very largely on its manipulation. Very often a collar that will not lie in the proper line will do so if its upper edge is waved. The shaping of the head-dresses is worth much labour. One point may be emphasized. The modern woman, left to herself, will invariably put them too far down on her forehead, with disastrous results. (Quite why, I do not know, but the effect, if nothing else, is somehow vulgar.) She will probably be distinctly peevish, too, when they are lifted, and swear that the result is unbecoming. If you have a long mirror, you can prove to her that *with the rest of her Elizabethan costume,* it is not, especially if she has at all a decent profile: if you have no mirror you must make her take your word for it. It matters. The characteristic poise of the head-dress may be difficult to get, especially on a shingled head, but it is worth some labour. If veils are attached to the caps (and they are most dignified and decorative) they should never be muslin. It is far too clumsy. Tulle,

unless it is old, is little better. The best thing is either *old*
tulle or chiffon, or what is cheaper than either, surgical gauze
bought at the chemist's. It can be dyed, but the frail floating
white goes well with most things.

Weight has a lot to do with successful drapery. A heavy
fringe to a scarf, tailor's leads in the points of a cloak or heavy
metal sequins in its border, thick tassels on hanging sleeves,
may make all the difference between good line and bad.

I have spoken of glitter before. Don't be afraid of it: and
remember that anything that will sparkle can be made to look
like a jewel. An ancient bit of sequin trimming, particularly
red or green, an old paste shoebuckle with half the stones
out, a scrap of damaged diamanté from the sales, are most
effective. The last, indeed, has endless possibilities, not only
for necklaces and girdles, but sewn in short lengths on a round
of silk-covered cardboard with a safety-pin, it makes brooches
for ruff, corsage, and bonnet. A scrap of sequin on an elastic
band makes a ring that will *point* gesture as well as a five-
hundred-guinea diamond. And it is amazing what you can
do for half a crown (in Woolworth's) in the way of the orient
pearls Gloriana loved so.

To the amateur I may add also that if you cannot hire or
make Elizabethan costumes – and they are not easy for the
home dressmaker – you may have to fall back on mediæval,
Greek (in some plays) or merely fancy dress. Greek is the
easiest if it is cut properly: that is, with everything rectangular. And unbleached cotton with the dressing washed
out of it has the warm white of wool. It is cheap, too: I
produced *Midsummer Night's Dream* in Greek dress once,
and the whole production (we had our hall for nothing) cost
nine pounds and was very good to look at, though I should in
fairness add that we were much helped by the generous loan

of some beautiful shawls. But Greek is only possible in a few plays, and I do not think it is really best for any. Mediæval, in a history, should at least attempt to follow the real period, and should be consistent in general effect (there is a lot of difference between thirteenth and fifteenth century) though there is no need to be archæologically priggish. If the play is of no period in particular the best thing to aim at is an Italian Quattrocento[1] effect: it fits the atmosphere next best to Elizabethan. But even the next best is a long way after. The merely fanciful is best avoided, unless you are sure that your designer is a genius: and then he will probably avoid it himself.

Lighting, scene, costume, are important things. But more important than any is the acting. And the first point here is imagination, and the second speech. In almost any Elizabethan play worthy revival, the poetry is one of the things that matter: and a man with no ear for the rhythm of the great decasyllable will mangle Marlowe or Webster as surely as a man with no ear for pitch will mangle Byrd. It is no good attempting to be too 'natural.' Blank verse is not 'natural' – in the sense of 'normal' – speech. Sometimes it approaches to it, especially in rapid dialogue, or in the later plays: and then, of course, should be treated more or less naturalistically – the precise degree depends upon many things. But the long declamatory speeches are meant to be declaimed as verse, and should be. This does not mean, of course, that they should be bellowed. And distinct clear-cut enunciation of both consonants and vowels is the first and primary element of the actor's art.

[1] *Il quattrocento,* of course, is what in English usage we would call the *fifteenth* century.

It is unnecessary to say that movement ought to be expressive, and where grotesquerie is not demanded, comely. But I am forced to mention one point which should be equally unneeded. The actor of Elizabethan plays must learn to carry his clothes, including a man's sword or a woman's skirt, and look at home in them. The skirt is as important as the sword, for few people nowadays are 'broke' to trains, and I have seen a well-known actress, playing Webster, look as awkward in hers as a policeman in a crinoline. Illusion perishes, and poetry along with it, when your cast are too obviously twentieth-century folk in fancy-dress. From some painful experience I very strongly recommend all producers – professional as well as amateur – to make their players wear swords and trains at rehearsals. One dress rehearsal, even the two that there certainly ought to be, is inadequate to make most people look at home in them, and if a man has rehearsed a love-scene for weeks with a lady in a knee-length skirt, he may be very badly worried on 'the night' when he finds he has to keep his feet out of a couple of square yards of moving velvet, and avoid getting his sword between his legs. It is not necessary to wear costume with them: a length of bamboo, or better still, a foil, slung on with string or pendant from an old Sam Browne, a dust-sheet pinned about the waist, are all that is needed. The sword, incidentally, gives a man something to do with his hand: a woman can use a fan for the same purpose. Again (and once more I speak from bitter experience) the men should always rehearse with hats. Otherwise the hero will outrage Elizabethan – or modern – courtesy by forgetting to remove his hat at the King's entrance, or in the heroine's apartment. I have seen a good professional actor make this very blunder.

These may seem trivial details. But they count. And it

does not take much trouble to avoid some ugly but common errors of the sort.

Grouping is less the actor's affair than the producer's, and one who is any good at all will not forget the admirable decorative effects of pose and arrangement, and how – especially with splendour of dress to help them – they can be made most vitally significant. But one opportunity is seldom taken – the possibilities of the procession. Of course if the producer is a Catholic, he will not need to be reminded of that ordered stately beauty: and the use of it in drama is legitimate, for it was a regular device of Elizabethan managers, whose characters *must* enter in view of the audience, and who therefore made them do so in state, to the sound of trumpets, and take their places as in a pavane. Such an entrance 'gets the atmosphere' before a word of dialogue is spoken. And a withdrawal in the same fashion may have a deep emotional significance. When a procession, such as a wedding or a funeral, is part of the action, it should be treated as a scene, not huddled anyhow across the stage. It is extraordinary what trifling means will give a sense of pomp, if rightly handled.

Another, and important point, is speed. For all the dignity of its serious side, the Elizabethan drama is meant to be played rapidly. This does not mean that speeches should be gabbled. But they must follow each other as swift as parry and riposte, and scene must come on scene with equal promptness. Long waits between will cool the atmosphere disastrously, and make a bored and apathetic audience. The Elizabethan performance was over in two hours.

One interval, at the most, should be enough. Every time the lights in the auditorium are turned on, the temperature

of the audience has to be worked up again from zero. Much
of the speed depends on the discipline of the company behind
the scenes. The amateur one needs a competent call-boy,
and is wise to rehearse, if it can, with its scene-shifters.

Music is not in my province: but I will end here with a
word at least on noise. If you are going to make a noise,
make it. There is no use in Othello ordering 'Silence that
dreadful bell: it frights the isle!' in front of a mild tinkle that
would hardly reach the gallery. I have seen a well-known
Shakespearian company ruin one of the most dramatic effects
in *Macbeth* by an 'alarum-bell' that, instead of crashing
through the low-voiced talk like the trump of doom, would
hardly have disturbed a sleeping kitten. Shakespeare knew
well, and often used, the emotional value of a sudden loud
sound 'off': but it is one of the points where producers often
let him down.

To conclude these very rambling but I hope not useless
dicta, may I offer to anyone who produces an Elizabethan
play not only the sincere and heartfelt sympathy that I extend
to all producers whatsoever, but my warmest good wishes and
the assurance that, successful or not, he will find it very well
worth while.

APPENDIX I

CHRONOLOGICAL TABLES

N.B.—Most of the literary chronology of this period is rather vague, and that of the drama is especially so. A few definite and ascertained dates are given to serve as milestones: the others as a rule are not intended to be anything more than probable approximations.

10th century.	Early liturgical plays.
11th and 12th.	Early Mystery and Miracle Plays.
13th.	These are passing to lay actors.
14th and 15th.	Rise of Moralities.
1500–1550.	Mystery, Miracle, and Morality still popular.
	Rise of Masque and Interlude.

Elizabeth born 1533.

1550–1560.	All the above still popular.
	Ralph Roister Doister. Gammer Gurton. King Johan.
	Lyly, Peele, Greene, Chapman, born.

Elizabeth's accession 1558.

1560–1570.	Drama of mediæval type still popular.
	Classical influence strengthens. *Gorboduc,* 1562.
	Many secular plays, now lost.
	Kyd born. Marlowe and Shakespeare born, 1564.

**Mary arrives in Scotland 1561, deposed
1567.**

1570–1580.   Drama of mediæval type still played, but
new kinds ousting it.

The Theatre built 1576, followed by other
playhouses.

Jonson, Marston, Heywood, Dekker, Middleton, Fletcher, born.

1580–1590.   Nearly all the work of the University
Wits.

Lyly and Peele begin 1584.

Marlowe's *Tamburlaine* 1586–7

Kyd's *Spanish Tragedy*, c. 1587.

Shakespeare begins to revise old plays, c.
1587. Writes *L.L.L.*, *T.G.V.*, *C.o.E.*,
T.o.S.

Beaumont, Massinger, ?Webster, ?Ford
born.

1590–1595.   Shakespeare's work still largely experi-
mental: includes *M.N.D.*, *R. and J.*,
John, *R.II.*, *R.III.*, *A.W.*, *M.o.V*

Last work of the Wits.

Greene died 1592, Marlowe 1593.

1595–1600.   Shakespeare, *Hy. IV.*, *Hy. V.*, *M.W.W.*,
A.Y., *M.A.*

Jonson beginning. Lost plays. *Every Man
in his Humour. Every Man out of his
Humour.*

Chapman beginning. *Blind Beggar of Alexandria. An Humorous Day's Mirth.*

Heywood beginning. *Four Prentices. Four
Ages. Edward IV.*

Dekker beginning. *Shoemakers' Holiday.
Old Fortunatus.*

Peele died, ?1579.

1600–1605.   Shakespeare turning to tragedy: *T.N., J.C.,
T. and C., Hamlet, M.f.M., Othello.*

Jonson, *Cynthia's Revels, Poetaster, Sejanus, Volpone* 1605.

Chapman, *All Fools.* Probably some lost
plays also.

Marston (may have begun a little earlier).
*Antonio and Mellida, Revenge of Antonio,
Malcontent* 1605.

Eastward Ho 1604.

Dekker, *Patient Grissil, The Honest Whore,*
etc.

Heywood, *A Woman Killed with Kindness,
Lucrece,* etc.

Middleton beginning. *Mayor of Queenborough, Blurt Master Constable.*

Rowley, with Middleton in *Mayor,* etc.
Perhaps also alone.

Other minors.

James' accession, 1603.

1605–1610.   Shakespeare's tragedies continue: he turns
to comedy again. *T.o.A., Lear, Macbeth,
A. and C., P.P.T., Cor., Cym.*

Jonson. Masques begin 1605. *Silent
Woman* 1609. *Alchemist* 1610.

Chapman, *Bussy d'Amboise* 1607. *Con-
spiracy of Biron, Tragedy of Biron* 1608.

Marston gave up theatre 1607.

Dekker writing: plays impossible to date and many lost.

Heywood, ? *Fortune by Land and Sea*? *Fair Maid of the West*,? *A Challenge for Beauty*, etc.

Middleton,? *A Chaste Maid in Cheapside*, etc.

Rowley working, largely in collaboration.

Tourneur, *Revenger's Tragedy*, *Atheist's Tragedy*.

Webster beginning. Lost plays. *White Devil*, 1607.

Beaumont and Fletcher beginning. *Woman Hater* 1607, *Faithful Shepherdess*, *Kt. of Burning Pestle*, *Scornful Lady*.

Minors.

1610–1615.   Shakespeare's last work. *W.T.*, *Tempest*. *Hy.VIII.* with Fletcher Jan. 1613.

Jonson, *Catiline*, 1611, *Bartholomew Fair* 1614, masques.

Chapman, *May Day*, *The Widow's Tears*, *Revenge of Bussy d'Amboise* 1613.

Dekker, *The Roaring Girl*, etc.

Heywood writing.

Middleton writing.

Rowley writing.

Webster, *The Duchess of Malfi* 1614.

Beaumont and Fletcher, *A King and no King*, *Maid's Tragedy*, *Philaster*, *M. Thomas*, *Valentinian*, *Bonduca*, *Bloody Brother*.

Minors.

1615–1620.   Shakespeare died 1616. Beaumont same year.

Jonson, lost plays.

Middleton and Rowley, *A Fair Quarrel, The Changeling*, etc.

Webster, *Devil's Law Case, Appius and Virginia.*

Fletcher, *Thierry and Theodoret, Two Noble Kinsmen*, etc.

Massinger beginning. ?*Virgin Martyr* (with Dekker), ?*Duke of Milan.*

Numerous minors, mostly of school of B. and F.

1620–1630.   Fletcher died 1625. Middleton 1627.

Jonson, lost plays.

Heywood probably writing still, but plays lost.

Fletcher, *Wild Goose Chase, Spanish Curate, Rule a Wife and Have a Wife.*

Massinger, *A New Way to Pay Old Debts, Roman Actor, Maid of Honour, Great Duke of Florence*, etc.

Ford beginning, *Lover's Melancholy, Broken Heart, Love's Sacrifice, 'Tis Pity She's a Whore.*

Shirley beginning.

Numerous minors.

Accession of Charles 1633.

1630–1640.   Chapman and Marston died 1634. Jonson 1637. Dekker *c.* 1637. Massinger 1640. Heywood still living in 1640.

Massinger writing.
Ford writing.
Shirley writing (lived to 1666).
Numerous minors, some of whom lived
well into Restoration period.

Theatres closed 1642-1660.

APPENDIX II

THE BRITISH DRAMA LEAGUE

THE BRITISH DRAMA LEAGUE, 8 Adelphi Terrace, W.C.2, has for aim 'to assist the development of the art of the theatre, and to promote a right relationship between drama and the life of the community.' Membership of the League is open to 'all persons who are concerned with the practice or enjoyment of the art of the theatre,' and may be acquired by the payment of an annual subscription of £1 1s. Any organized society or group of not less than ten persons may become affiliated to the League, and as an affiliated body shall acquire and exercise all the privileges afforded by the League. The minimum affiliation fee is £1 1s. There is an annual conference. The League will advise on all matters concerning the production of plays, and will also criticize plays written by members. It possesses an excellent small library of books relating to the drama. Individual members may borrow three books at once without further subscription. Societies paying more than £1 1s. in subscription are entitled to borrow books and sets of plays in proportion to their subscription. Sets of plays (one copy for each character up to twelve) may be hired for 2s. 6d. for one week and 5s. for longer periods up to six weeks. The League produces a monthly magazine, *Drama*, which is sent free to all members.

APPENDIX III

THE PHŒNIX SOCIETY AND THE RENAISSANCE THEATRE

THE PHŒNIX SOCIETY, 36 Southampton Street, W.C.2, and The Renaissance Theatre, Adelphi Hotel, Adam Street, W.C.2, exist for the production of older English plays by companies of professional actors and actresses. Membership is open to all persons interested in the drama. The terms of annual subscription are, for the Phœnix Society, £4 4s. for two seats for each production (three to five in the season) in stalls or dress circle, £2 12s. 6d. for one such seat, or for two seats in the upper circle or pit, and £1 1s. for two seats for each production in the gallery. For the Renaissance Theatre, which performs foreign plays as well as English, the terms are from £3 3s. for two stalls or dress circle seats for each production to 15s. for two gallery seats for such production. The pre-Restoration plays produced by the Phœnix Society are (1919) *The Duchess of Malfi*, (1920) *The Fair Maid of the West*, (1921) *Volpone, The Witch of Edmonton, Bartholomew Fair, The Maid's Tragedy*, (1922) *The Chances, The Jew of Malta*, (1923) *'Tis Pity She's a Whore, The Alchemist, The Faithful Shepherdess, Edward II*, (1924) *King Lear, The Silent Woman*, (1925) *Doctor Faustus*. There were also ten productions of Restoration plays. The Renaissance Theatre has produced, (1925) *Rule a Wife and Have a Wife, The Maid's Tragedy, The Wild Goose Chase, Arden of Feversham* and *The White Devil*, besides plays by Wycherly, Molière, and Calderon.

APPENDIX IV

AMATEUR PRODUCTIONS

It has unfortunately been found impossible to offer any record of amateur productions of Elizabethan and Jacobean plays, though of recent years these have been fairly numerous. The pioneers were probably the Elizabethan Stage Society, founded in 1895 to produce Elizabethan plays as nearly as possible under Elizabethan conditions. One gathers from contemporary reports that the simplicity of staging did not always secure an undismembered version of the play: nevertheless, the Society gave a valuable lead. Its pre-Restoration productions were *Twelfth Night* in 1895, 1897, and 1903, *The Comedy of Errors* in 1895, *Faustus* in 1896, *The Two Gentlemen of Verona* in 1897 and 1910, *The Tempest* in 1897, *Edward III* and scenes from *Arden of Feversham* in 1897, *The Coxcomb*, *The Spanish Gipsy*, *The Broken Heart* and *The Sad Shepherd* in 1898, *The Merchant of Venice* in 1898 and 1907, *The Alchemist* in 1899 and 1902, *Richard II* in 1899, *Hamlet* in the First Quarto Version in 1900, *Henry V* in 1901, *Edward II* in 1902, *Much Ado about Nothing* in 1904, *Romeo and Juliet* in 1905, *Measure for Measure* in 1908, *Macbeth* in 1909, and *Troilus and Cressida* in 1912. More recently, typical achievements are those of the Maddermarket Theatre, Norwich, a brilliant company of amateurs whose widely ranging work includes *The May Lady*, *The Yorkshire Tragedy*, *The Duchess of Malfi*, *A New Way to Pay Old Debts*, and twenty-three plays of Shakespeare; the Cambridge University Marlowe Society, which has produced *Doctor Faustus*, *A New Way to Pay Old Debts*, *The Silent Woman*, *Richard II*, *The Knight of the Burning Pestle*, *The Alchemist*, *Henry IV, 1*, *The White Devil*, *The Triumph*

177   M

of Death, *Arden of Feversham*, *Troilus and Cressida*, *Volpone*, *The Duchess of Malfi*, and *Edward II*. The Literary Society of Birkbeck College (University of London) produced the following between 1919 and 1925: *The Old Wife's Tale*, *Friar Bacon and Friar Bungay*, *Edward II*, *The Spanish Tragedy*, *Sir Thomas More* (first performance on any stage!) *Arden of Feversham*, *The Case is Altered*, *Philaster*. On a less ambitious scale, The Newport Playgoers' Society, Monmouthshire, have read *Campaspe*, *Faustus*, *Ralph Roister Doister*, *Antony and Cleopatra*, and *The Silent Woman*.

NOTE. – An Australian correspondent was good enough to send me the following information. Between 1920 and 1924 Mr. Allan Wilkie's Company presented in Australia no fewer than twenty of Shakespeare's plays. Mr. Wilkie (who has also founded a *Shakespearian Quarterly*) had hoped to produce the whole of them, but was hindered by a disastrous fire. Writing in London, which has a greater population than the whole Australian continent, I am interested to know that Mr. Wilkie has declared, 'In Hobart (Tasmania), with its population of 60,000, I can always play an annual season of at least a month to good houses throughout.' The Mermaid Play Society (amateurs) of Melbourne, later the Melbourne Repertory Theatre, have produced, in addition to four plays of Shakespeare, *Everyman*, *The Interlude of Youth*, and *The Knight of the Burning Pestle*.

APPENDIX V
SOME USEFUL BOOKS

TEXTS

THE Mermaid Series (Fisher Unwin) contains a selection of from two to six plays apiece from the works of the more important Jacobean and Elizabethan dramatists. The selection is not always of the best plays, and many of the introductions have 'dated' badly, but the series still remains the most convenient for the general reader. Dent's Everyman series contains the complete dramatic works of Marlowe and Jonson (the latter in two volumes), selections from Beaumont and Fletcher (six plays), two volumes of Minor Elizabethan Drama (Tragedies: *Gorboduc, David and Bethsabe, Arden of Feversham, The Spanish Tragedy*. Comedies: *Ralph Roister Doister, Endymion, The Old Wife's Tale, Friar Bacon, James IV*) and a volume of representative mystery and morality plays. The Temple Series (same publishers) contains a good many single plays, carefully edited. Mr. W. A. Neilson's *The Chief Elizabethan Dramatists* (pub. Harrap) is a single volume containing thirty plays, from *Endymion* to *The Cardinal*.

HISTORY AND CRITICISM

Bradley, A. C., *Shakespearian Tragedy*. Macmillan.

> Perhaps the greatest book that has been written about Shakespeare.

Chambers, E. K., *The Elizabethan Stage*. 4 vols. Clarendon Press.

> A monument of scholarship, embodying all the known facts of Elizabethan stage history.

Coleridge, S. T., *Lectures on Shakespeare*. Everyman Series.

> A study of a dramatist and psychologist by a man who was neither — but also, a study of one great poet by another.

Hamilton, C. M., *The Theory of the Theatre*. Holt.

> The chapters on Economy of Attention and Emphasis are valuable to actors and producers.

Hazlitt, W., *Characters of Shakespeare's Plays*. Everyman.
  Shakespeare and *Jonson*, in *The English Comic Writers*. Everyman.
  Have the defects of their age, and the gusto and brilliance of their writer.

Herford, C. H. ed., *Shakespeare's England*. 2 vols. Oxford University Press.
  'An Handful of Pleasant Delights,' and a treasury of information as to the life of the period. Essays on (Vol. I) The Age of Elizabeth, Religion, the Court, the Soldier, Armour and Weapons, Ships and Sailors, Voyages and Explorations, Maps, Land-Travel, Education, Scholarship, Handwriting, Commerce and Coinage, Agriculture and Gardening, Law, Medicine, the Sciences, Folklore, Witchcraft, etc. (Vol. II) The Fine Arts, Heraldry, Costume, Furniture, Food, Domestic Customs, London and its Life, Authors and Patrons, Booksellers, Printers, Actors, the Playhouse, the Masque, Sports, incl. Fencing and the Duel, Rogues and Vagabonds, Ballads and Broadsides, Shakespeare's English.

Lee, Sidney, *Life of Shakespeare*, 2 vols. Smith and Elder.
  The standard biography. One is aware of monumental scholarship, with a temperamental barrier between author and subject.

Mantzius, Karl, *History of Theatrical Art*, Vol. III. Eng. tr. Duckworth.
  A classic work of reference, by a man who was both scholar and actor.

Matthews, Brander, *Playwrights and Playmaking*. Scribner.
  Essay on Undramatic Criticism should be borne in mind by all teachers and critics.

Montague, C. E., *Dramatic Values*. Methuen.
>   A wise and stimulating little book.

Poel, W., *Shakespeare in the Theatre*. Sidgwick and Jackson.
>   Mr. Poel has done much to bring Elizabethan drama
>   to life again, in its proper place on the stage.

Quiller Couch, A., *Shakespeare's Workmanship*. Oxford
University Press.
>   A wise and human book, by a critic who can enter
>   the experience of the creative artist.

Raleigh, W., *Shakespeare*. English Men of Letters Series.
>   Biographical and critical. Less full than Lee's, but
>   with much more of Shakespeare's personality in it. A
>   good introduction.

Schelling, F. E., *English Drama*. Dent.
>   A sound standard history of the subject in one volume.

Symonds, J. A., *Shakespeare's Predecessors in English Drama*.
Smith and Elder.
>   Fascinating descriptive and analytic criticism.

Temple, W., *Mens Creatrix*. Macmillan.
>   The chapter on Tragedy might well be read in con-
>   junction with Bradley.

Ward, A. W., *English Dramatic Literature*. 3 vols. Macmillan.
>   Substantial and well-documented scholarship.

Ward, A. W. and Walker, A. R., ed. *Cambridge History of
English Literature*, Vols. V and VI. Cambridge
University Press.
>   (Vol. V). A. W. Ward, Origins of English Drama:
>   H. H. Child, Secular Influences on Early English
>   Drama: W. Creizenach, Early Religious Drama: J. W.
>   Cunliffe, Early English Tragedy: F. S. Boas, Early
>   English Comedy: G. P. Baker, The University Wits:

G. G. Smith, Marlowe and Kyd: G. Saintsbury,
Shakespeare: F. W. Moorman, Shakespeare Apocrypha:
E. Waldes, Text of Shakespeare: F. G. Robertson,
Shakespeare on the Continent: A. W. Ward, Some
political and social aspects of the late Elizabethan period
(Vol. VI). A. H. Thorndike, Ben Jonson: W. M
Dixon, Chapman, Marston, Dekker: A. Symon, Mid-
dleton and Rowley: A. W. Ward, Heywood: G. C.
Macaulay, Beaumont and Fletcher: E. Koeppel, Mas-
singer: C. E. Vaughan, Tourneur and Webster: W. A.
Neilson, Ford and Shirley: R. Bayne, Jacobean and
Caroline Minors. H. Child, The Elizabethan Theatre:
J. M. Montz, Children of the Chapel Royal: F. S.
Boas, University Plays: R. Bayne, Masque and Pas-
toral: J. D. Wilson, The Puritan attack upon the Stage.

PRODUCTION AND SCENERY

Appia, A., *L'Œuvre d'art vivant*. Atar.
> Brilliantly suggestive, but deals mainly with abstract
> principles.

Gordon Craig, E., *The Art of the Theatre*. Heinemann.
> Narrow and extreme, but immensely stimulating.

Mitchell, R., *Shakespeare for Community Players*. Dent.
> Very practical, with full details of production, stag-
> ing, and properties. Rather shaky on costume, but
> otherwise valuable. Contains a list of settings of Shakes-
> peare's songs.

Smedley, Constance. *Production*. Duckworth.
> Small, but suggestive.

Vernon, F., *Modern Stage Production*. The Stage.
> Lays down sound general principles.

Weston Wells, H., *A Simple Stage for a Little Theatre.*
Article in *Drama* for October, 1926.
Directions and diagrams for what appears to be a
very effective 'curtain set.'

LIGHTING

Ridge, C. H., *Stage Lighting for the Little Theatre.* Heffer.
Recommended by the Drama League.

MAKE-UP

Chalmers, Helena, *The Art of Make-up.* Appleton.
Fitzgerald, S. J. A., *How to Make-up.* French.
Recommended by the Drama League.

COSTUME

Calthrop, D. C., *English Costume.* Black.
Good clear drawings.
Hughes, Talbot, *Dress Design.* Pitman.
Admirable illustrations, including such details as
shoes, etc., and photographs of actual garments. Work-
ing diagrams.
Kelly, F. M., and Schwabe, R. *Historic Costume.* Batsford.
Working drawings and many photographs of con-
temporary pictures.
Stone, Melicent, *The Bankside Costume Book.* Wells, Gard-
ner, Darton & Co.
Small, but very practical. Directions for making
costumes and accessories for any period required
in producing Shakespeare, including classical. Gives
armour, jewellery, and ecclesiastical and legal costume.
See also *Shakespeare's England.*

INDEX